Contents

☑ Use the tick boxes to help keep a record of which tests have been attempted.

Published by CGP

ISBN: 978 1 78908 828 1

Editors: Keith Blackhall, Tom Carney, Rachel Craig-McFeely, Emma Duffee
With thanks to Andy Cashmore and Juliette Green for the proofreading.
With thanks to Lottie Edwards for the copyright research.

Cover and Graphics used throughout the book © www.edu-clips.com

Printed by W&G Baird Ltd, Antrim.
Based on the classic CGP style created by Richard Parsons.

How to Use this Book

- This book contains <u>60 pages of daily spelling practice</u>.

- We've split them into <u>12 sections</u> — that's roughly one for <u>each week</u> of the Year 2 <u>Summer term</u>.

- Each week is made up of <u>5 pages</u>, so there's one for <u>every school day</u> of the term (Monday – Friday).

- Each page should take about <u>10 minutes</u> to complete.

- The words tested are suitable for the <u>Year 2</u> English curriculum. <u>New words</u> and <u>sounds</u> are gradually introduced through the book.

- The pages <u>increase in difficulty</u> as you progress through the book.

- <u>Answers</u> can be found at the <u>back</u> of the book.

- Each page looks something like this:

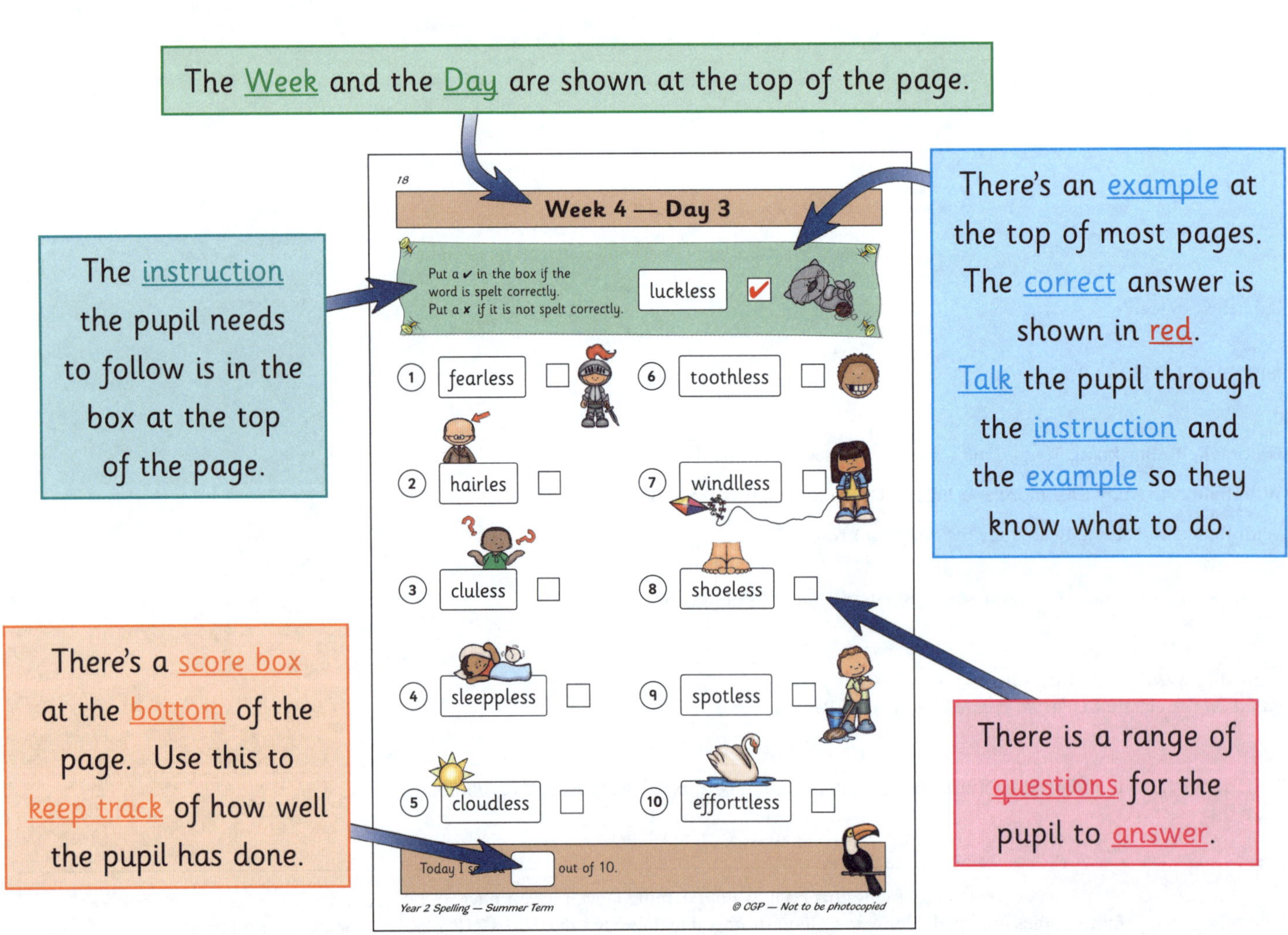

Week 1 — Day 1

Put a ✔ in the box if the word in bold is spelt correctly.
Put a ✘ if the word in bold is not spelt correctly.

Hamish is **riting** a story. ✘

1. It is about a **robot** called Bertie.

2. Bertie is in a **wrowing** contest.

3. He has to **race** down a river.

4. He is winning, but he takes a **wrong** turn.

5. Suddenly, he hits a big **wrock**!

6. Bertie's boat is **recked**.

7. Luckily, Bertie has a life **wraft**.

8. Hamish hasn't **written** the ending yet.

Today I scored [ ] out of 8.

Year 2 Spelling — Summer Term

Week 1 — Day 2

Look at the pictures. Circle the correct letters to complete each word.

boo__

c | **(k)** | s | ck

1 fa__e

c | k | s | ck

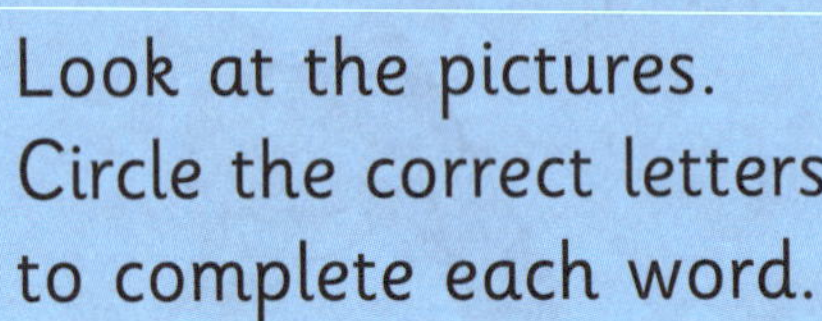

2 __ing

c | k | s | ck

3 dan__e

c | k | s | ck

4 sna__

c | k | s | ck

5 __ycle

c | k | s | ck

6 li__

c | k | s | ck

7 __astle

c | k | s | ck

8 prin__ess

c | k | s | ck

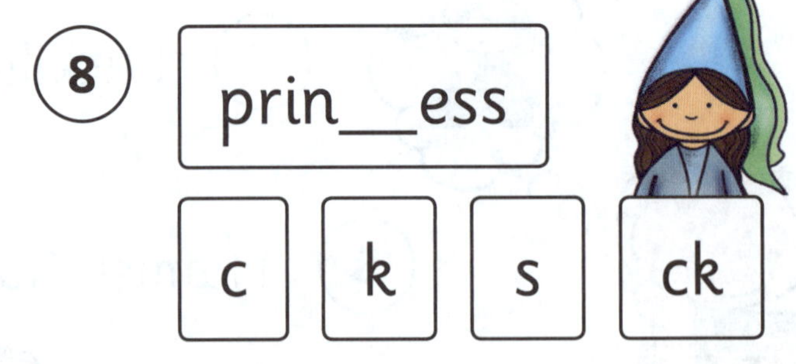

Today I scored ☐ out of 8.

Week 1 — Day 3

Keira is eating an **appil** / **apple** .

1. Mobo opens the **parcel** / **parcal** .

2. The **pupel** / **pupil** raises her hand.

3. The **eagil** / **eagle** flaps its wings.

4. A cheetah is a wild **animal** / **animil** .

5. Zosia **travels** / **travles** all over the world.

6. **Camals** / **Camels** live in the desert.

7. Joe wants to be a **jungle** / **jungil** explorer.

8. Imani finds a rare **fossal** / **fossil** .

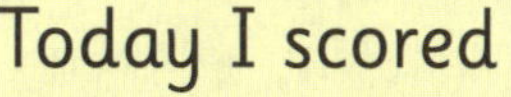

Today I scored [ ] out of 8.

Year 2 Spelling — Summer Term

Week 1 — Day 4

Look at the word in the first box. Write the correct spelling of the word when the suffix in the second box is added to it.

spike + y

spiky

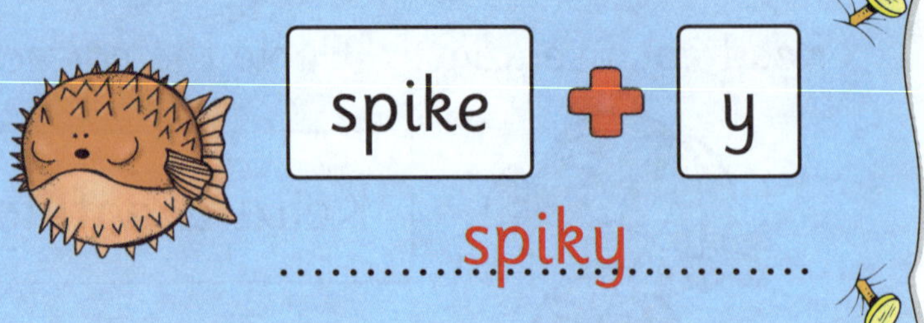

1. float + ed ....

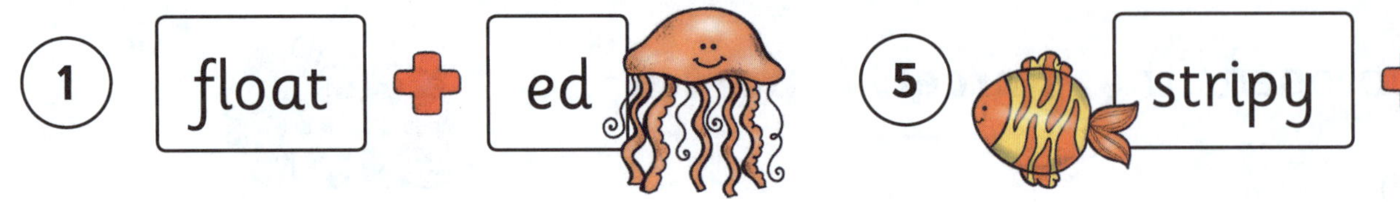

5. stripy + est ....

2. copy + ing ....

6. dive + er ....

3. spot + y ....

7. swim + ing ....

4. flip + er ....

8. study + ed ....

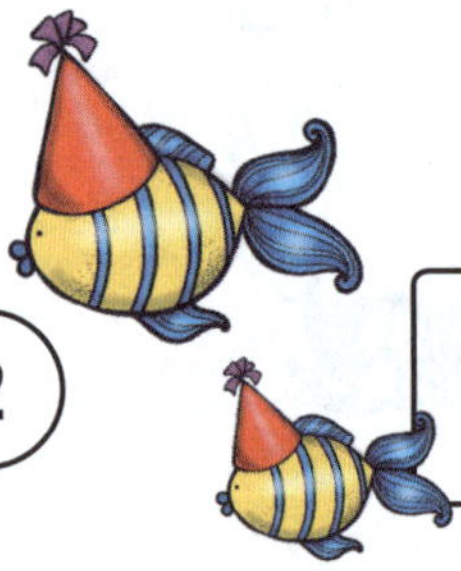

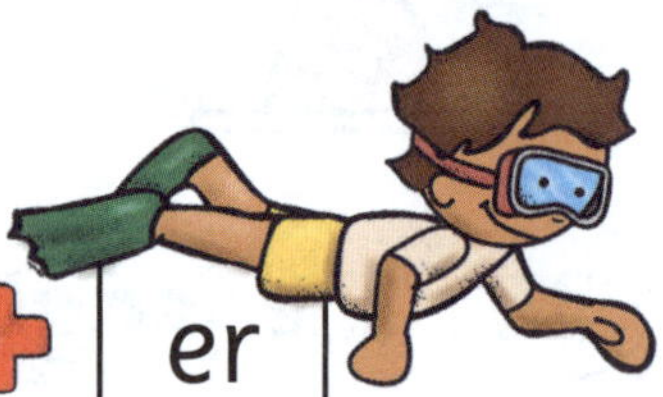

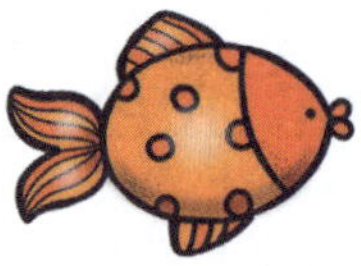

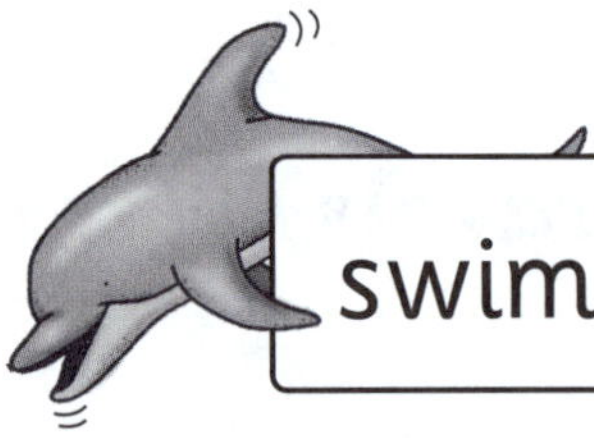

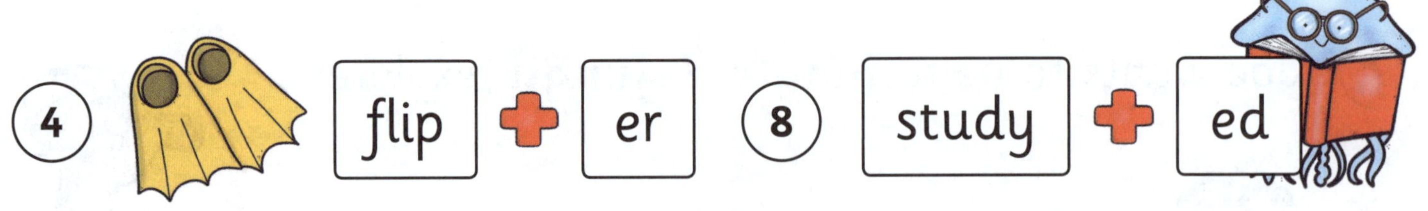

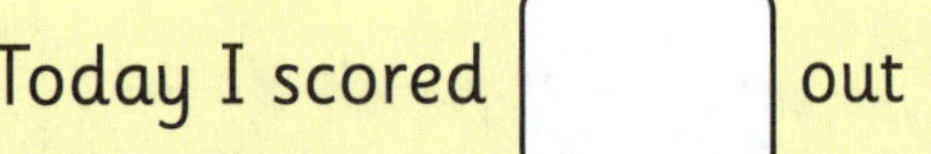

Today I scored [ ] out of 8.

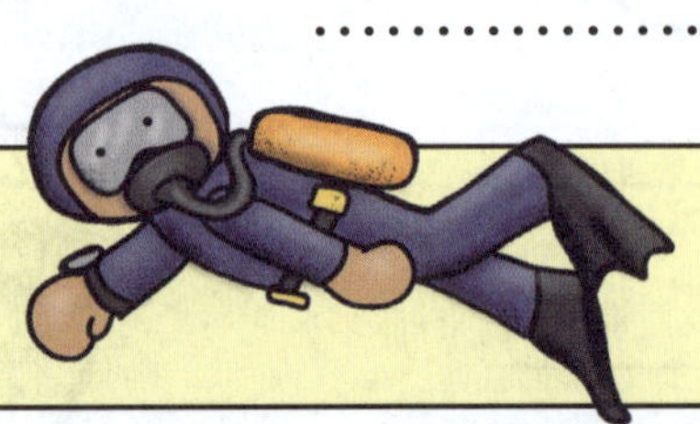

Week 1 — Day 5

Look at the picture. The sentences describe what is happening.
Add 'es' or 'ies' to the words in bold. Write the new word on the line.

1 Two **fox** are playing. ....

2 An owl sits in the **branch**. ....

3 A leaf **crunch** under Al's foot. ....

4 The tree is full of **berry**. ....

5 The **bush** have flowers. ....

6 The hedgehog has **baby**. ....

7 A bird **fly** through the air. ....

Today I scored [ ] out of 7.

Week 2 — Day 1

Colour the picture next to the word that is spelt correctly.

 muney | money 

1. 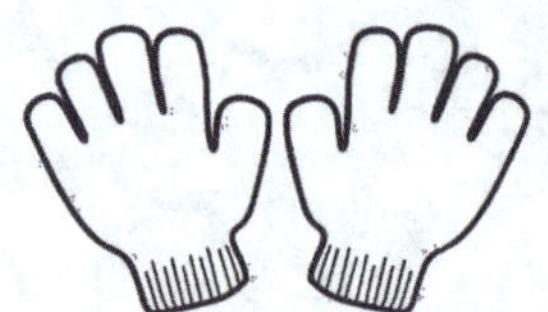 gluvs | gloves 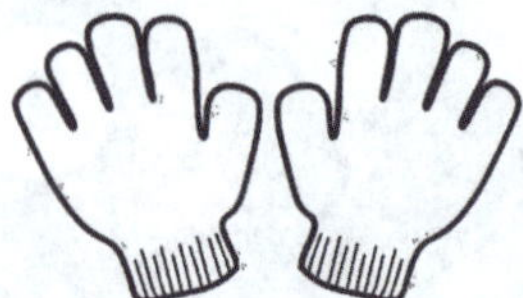

2.  mother | moother 

3.  funny | fonny 

4.  shov | shove 

5.  honey | huney 

6.  bruther | brother 

7. 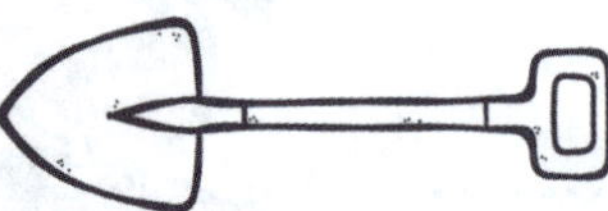 shuvl | shovel 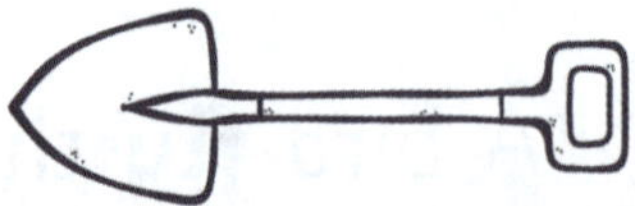

Today I scored [ ] out of 7. 

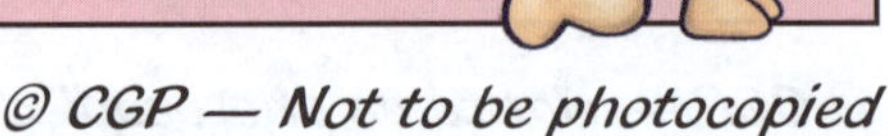

Week 2 — Day 2

Put a ✔ in the box if the word in bold is spelt correctly.
Put a ✘ if the word in bold is not spelt correctly.

Sara is going on a **journy**. ✘

1. It is warm and **sunney**. ☐

2. Sara walks through a green **valley**. ☐

3. There are lots of **donkees**. ☐

4. A **bunny** bounces past. ☐

5. Sara reaches the house with a **chimney**. ☐

6. She takes out her **keey**. ☐

7. When she opens the door, a **monky** greets her! ☐

8. It is not who she expected to **see**. ☐

Today I scored ☐ out of 8.

Year 2 Spelling — Summer Term

Week 2 — Day 3

Add either 'l' or 'll' to the words in bold to complete the sentences.

Polly is a......l....most forty.

1. She is **sma**........ and colourful.

2. She is **a**........**so** a parrot!

3. **A**........**though** Polly is quite old, she can still do a lot.

4. She can perform **a**........ sorts of amazing tricks.

5. She **ta**........**ks** and squawks loudly.

6. She can draw pictures with **cha**........**k**.

7. She **wa**........**ks** on her pointy claws.

8. Polly can even play **footba**........

Today I scored [ ] out of 8.

Week 2 — Day 4

Write the correct spelling of each word.

   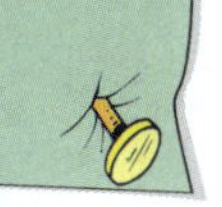

...... *wasps* ......

1  wond

....

2 warrn 

....

3  wosh

....

4 sqwat 

....

5  swon

....

6 quorter 

....

7  whatch

....

8  quorrel

....

Today I scored ☐ out of 8.

Year 2 Spelling — Summer Term

Week 2 — Day 5

Look at the pictures.
Fill in the missing letters
to correctly spell the word.

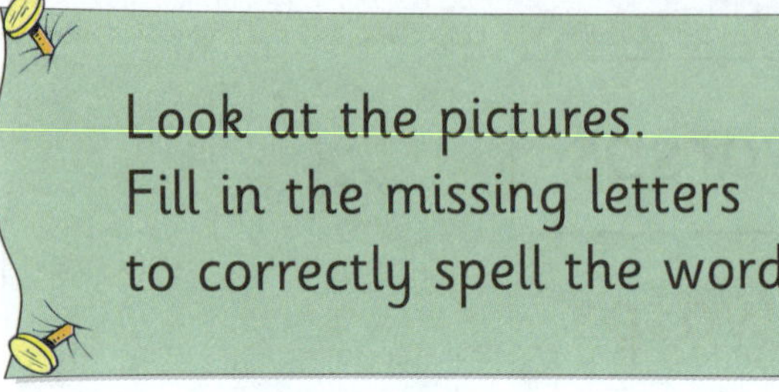

d ..w.. ..a.. r f

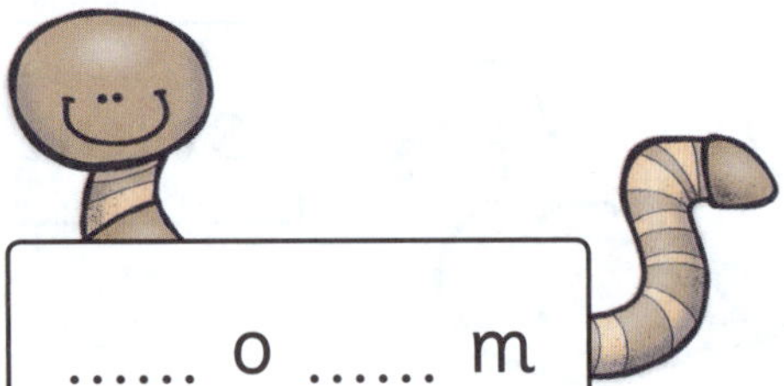

1 ..... o ..... m

2 w o ..... l .....

3 s ..... a ..... m

4 a w .... d

5 ..... a ..... m t h

6 .... r t h o g

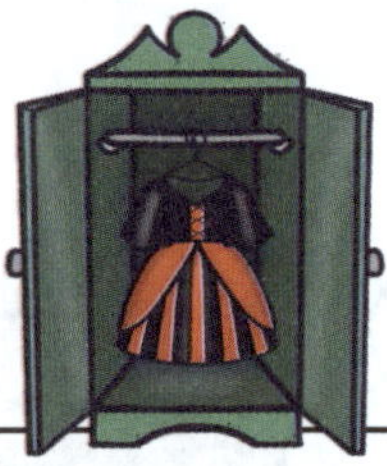

7 .... d r o b e

8 w .... s h ..... p

Today I scored [ ] out of 8.

Week 3 — Day 1

    Year 2 Spelling — Summer Term

Week 3 — Day 2

Read each sentence. Circle the correct spelling of the word in bold.

Hannah's **kindness** / **kindnes** is amazing.

(1) The **coldness** / **colddness** makes me shiver.

(2) Sid cannot shake his **tirednness** / **tiredness** .

(3) The drink has an odd **bitterness** / **biterness** .

(4) The **quiettness** / **quietness** is broken by a squawk.

(5) Zuko's **fluffiness** / **fluffyness** is well-known.

(6) We love his **friendlyness** / **friendliness** .

(7) I've never felt such **happiness** / **happyness** .

(8) The **roughness** / **roughnes** of the rock hurts my hand.

(9) His **sadness** / **saddness** lifted when he saw her.

Today I scored ☐ out of 9.

Week 3 — Day 3

Read each sentence. Write '**oi**' or '**oy**' to complete the words in bold.

Marcus likes playing with t....**oy**...s.

1 Cynthia found a shiny **c**..........**n**.

2 My dad has a **l**..........**al** dog called Otis.

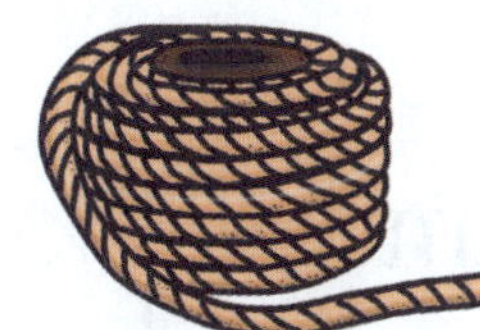

3 There was a **c**..........**l** of rope on the floor.

4 Bad weather **sp**..........**led** the barbecue.

5 "Stop **ann**..........**ing** your sister," said Mum.

6 The **r**..........**al** family live in an enormous castle.

7 Abeni has a lovely singing **v**..........**ce**.

8 Sasha's pet **tort**..........**se** can surf.

Today I scored ☐ out of 8.

Year 2 Spelling — Summer Term

Week 3 — Day 4

Write the correct spelling of each word when the suffix '**ment**' is added to it.

enjoy

enjoyment

1 agree 

....

2  refresh

....

3 punish 

....

4  equip

....

5 excite 

....

6  amuse

....

7 pave 

....

8  disappoint

....

Today I scored [ ] out of 8.

Week 3 — Day 5

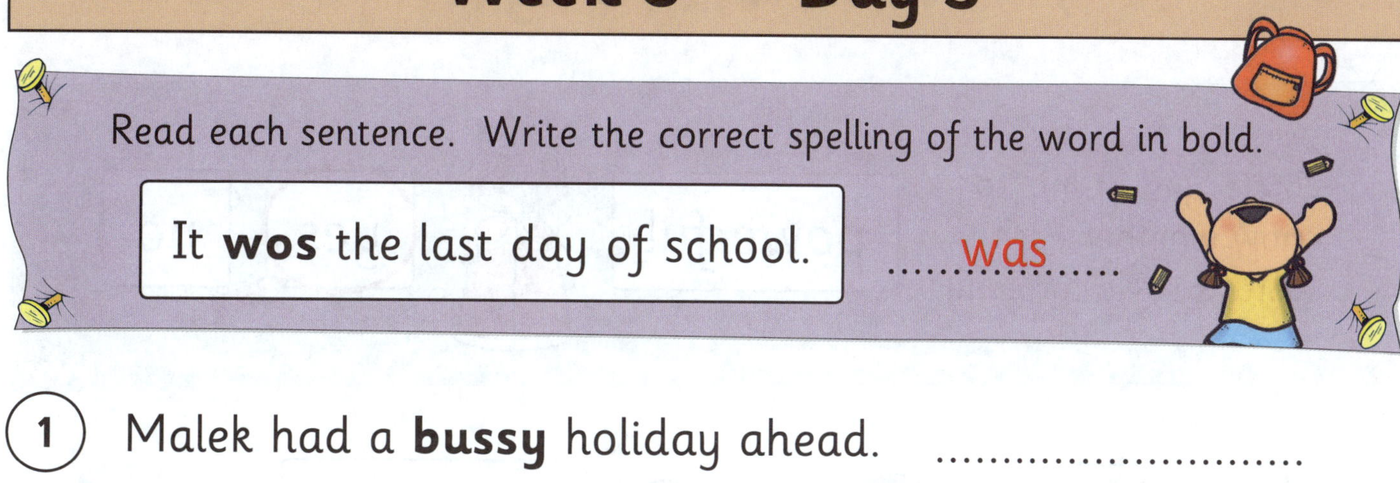

1. Malek had a **bussy** holiday ahead. ....

2. He had so **meny** plans! ....

3. He'd go to the **watur** park. ....

4. He'd play with his **frends**. ....

5. "Malek?" his teacher **caled** out. ....

6. "Are you listening?" she **asced**. ....

7. Malek **luked** confused. ....

8. The **clas** laughed. ....

9. "There's **won** day left!" his teacher said. ....

Today I scored [ ] out of 9.

Year 2 Spelling — Summer Term

Week 4 — Day 1

1 helpful

yes　no

2 lawfull

yes　no

3 graceful

yes　no

4 painnful

yes　no

5 beautyful

yes　no

6 cheerfful

yes　no

7 plentiful

yes　no

8 peacful

yes　no

Today I scored [ ] out of 8.

Week 4 — Day 2

Read each sentence. Circle the correct word in bold.

It is **Mareks** / **Marek's** birthday.

1. He is having a picnic at his **mum's** / **mums** house.

2. His **classmate's** / **classmates** come.

3. **Tarajis** / **Taraji's** dad brings lemonade.

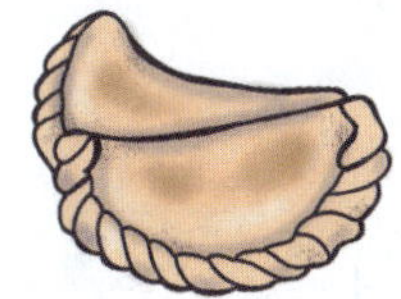

4. Harvey has made some **pastie's** / **pasties** .

5. **Kyle's** / **Kyles** biscuits are yummy.

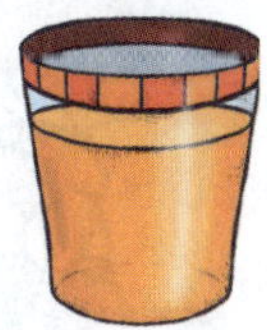

6. That juice is **Edwards** / **Edward's** .

7. Jasmine likes the **sandwiches** / **sandwich's** .

8. Granddad lights the **candle's** / **candles** .

Today I scored ☐ out of 8.

Week 4 — Day 3

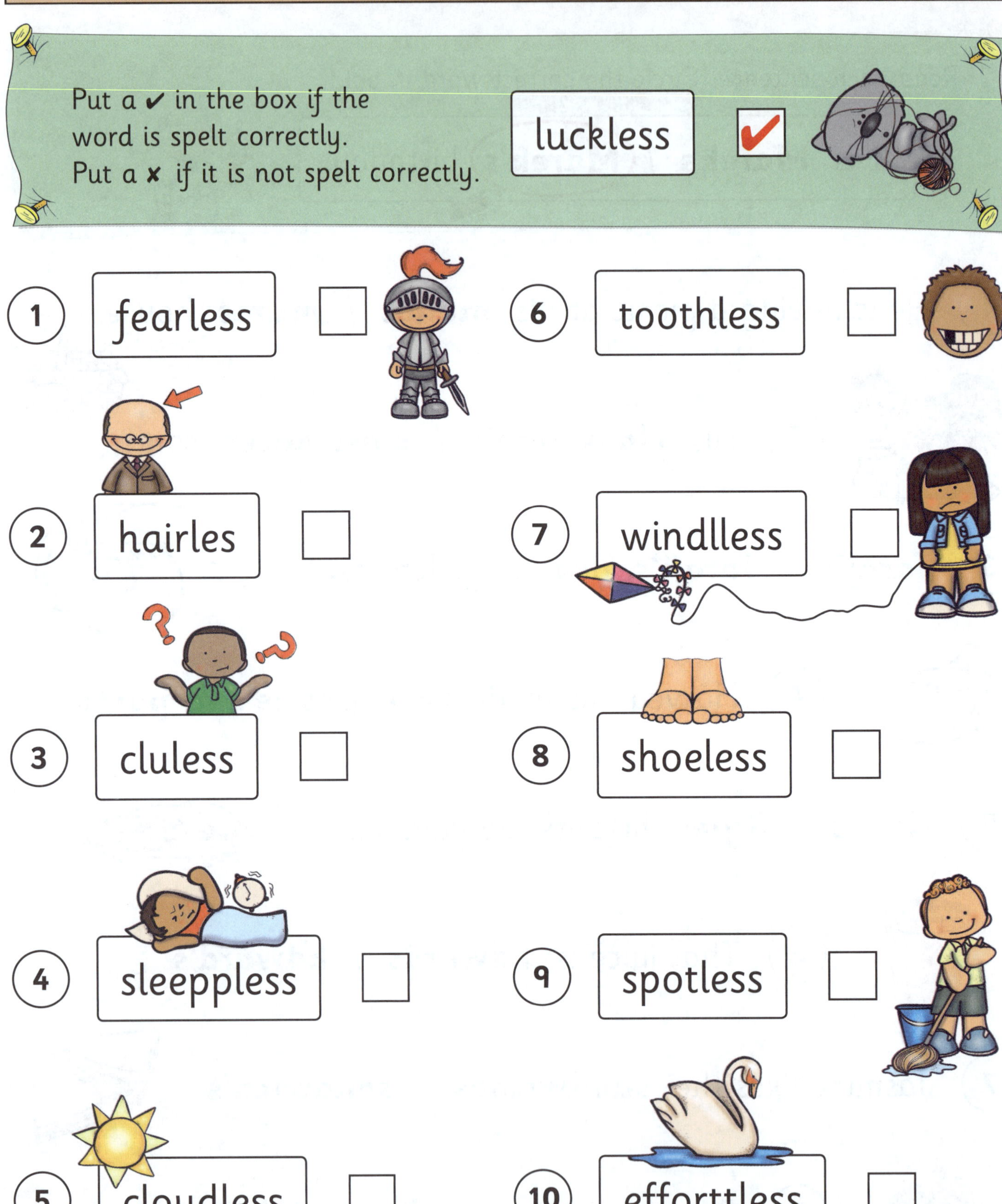

Put a ✔ in the box if the word is spelt correctly.
Put a ✘ if it is not spelt correctly.

luckless ✔

1. fearless ☐
2. hairles ☐
3. cluless ☐
4. sleeppless ☐
5. cloudless ☐
6. toothless ☐
7. windlless ☐
8. shoeless ☐
9. spotless ☐
10. efforttless ☐

Today I scored ☐ out of 10.

Week 4 — Day 4

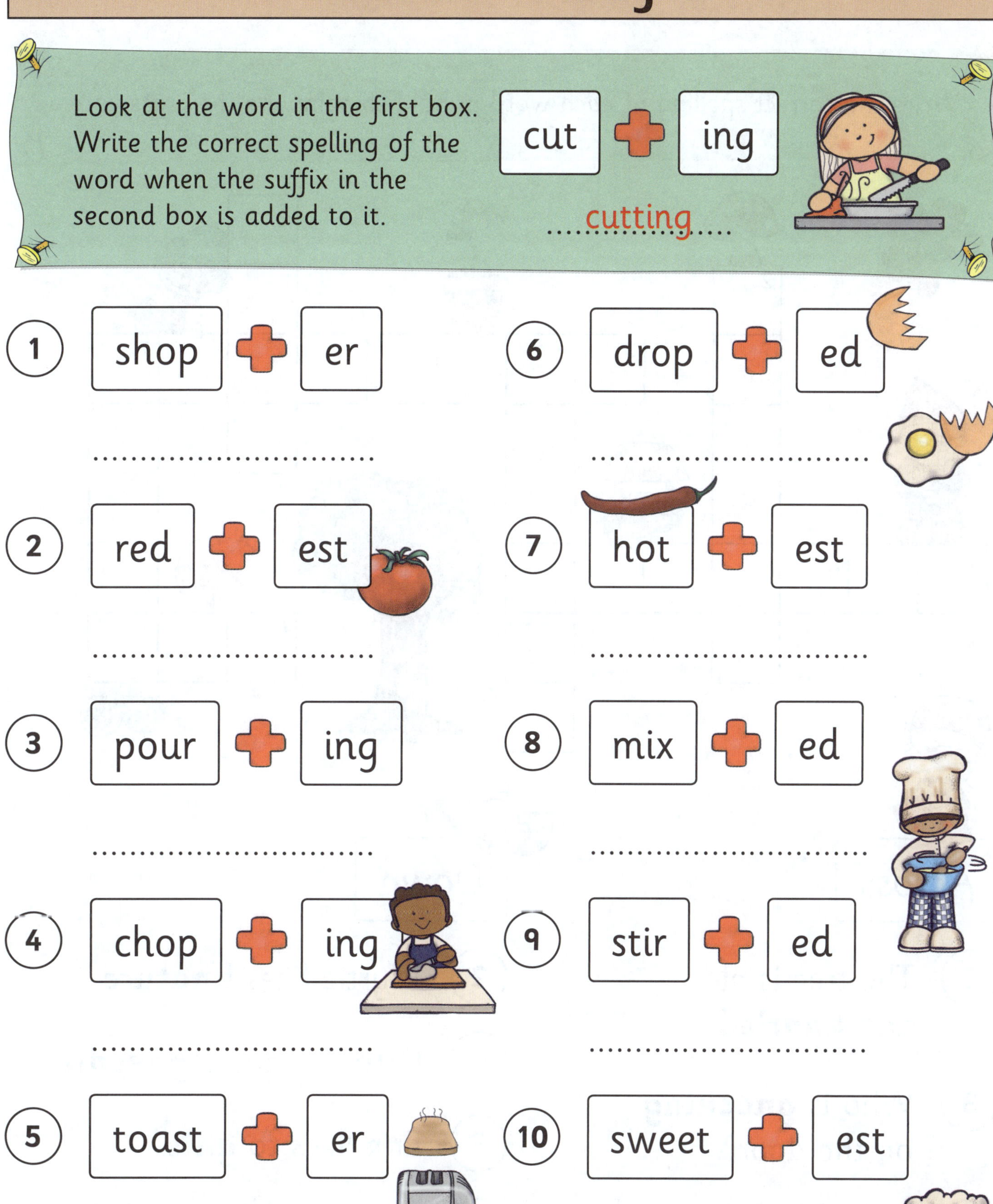

Look at the word in the first box. Write the correct spelling of the word when the suffix in the second box is added to it.

cut **+** ing

...cutting...

1. shop **+** er

....

2. red **+** est

....

3. pour **+** ing

....

4. chop **+** ing

....

5. toast **+** er

....

6. drop **+** ed

....

7. hot **+** est

....

8. mix **+** ed

....

9. stir **+** ed

....

10. sweet **+** est

....

Today I scored ____ out of 10.

   Year 2 Spelling — Summer Term

Week 4 — Day 5

Write the correct spelling of each word in bold to complete the crossword.

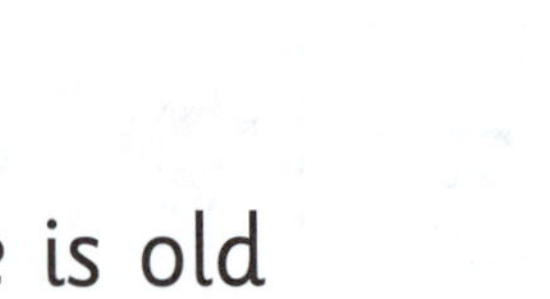

Across

1 The tree is old and **knarled**.

3 Who is **gnocking** on the door?

6 Giovanni hurt his **nee**.

Down

2 Myrtle likes **knature**.

4 Otto threads a **gneedle**.

5 Erik likes to **gnit**.

7 Nadia is a **nome**.

Today I scored [ ] out of 7.

Week 5 — Day 1

Read each pair of words. Put a **tick** in the box next to the word that is spelt correctly.

plezure ☐

pleasure ✔

1 measure ☐ / mesure ☐

2 lesur ☐ / leisure ☐

3 casual ☐ / cazual ☐

4 confuzion ☐ / confusion ☐

5 divijion ☐ / division ☐

6 occasion ☐ / ocassion ☐

7 inclusion ☐ / incluzion ☐

8 unuseual ☐ / unusual ☐

Today I scored ☐ out of 8.

Year 2 Spelling — Summer Term

Week 5 — Day 2

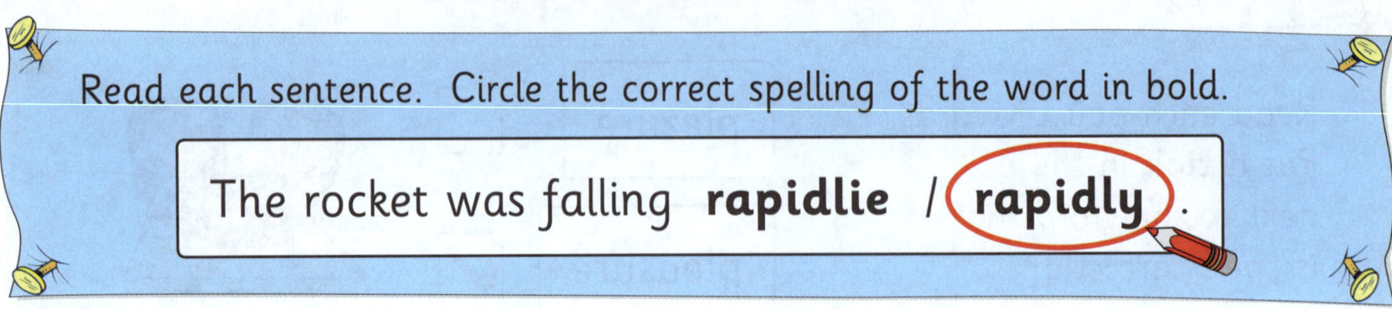

Read each sentence. Circle the correct spelling of the word in bold.

> The rocket was falling **rapidlie** / **rapidly** .

(1) "We must land **urgentli** / **urgently** !" said the Captain.

(2) They crashed **heavily** / **heavilee** on the planet.

(3) It was **nearly** / **nearli** a disaster.

(4) **Luckyly** / **Luckily** , no one was hurt.

(5) "Maybe we will find help," the Captain
    suggested **hopefully** / **hopefuly** .

(6) **Eventually** / **Eventuali** , they found some aliens.

(7) The aliens were **certainnly** / **certainly** helpful.

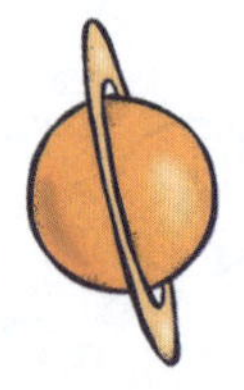

(8) They got the astronauts home **safly** / **safely** !

Today I scored ☐ out of 8.

Week 5 — Day 3

Colour the picture next to the word that is spelt correctly.

caution    caushon 

1 ficion    fiction 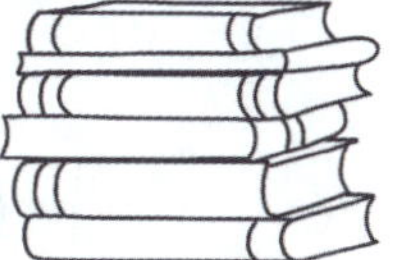

2 poshun    potion 

3 eruption    erupshun 

4 emoshin    emotion 

5 addition    additon 

6 question    questshun 

7 donation    donashon 

Today I scored [ ] out of 7.

Year 2 Spelling — Summer Term

Week 5 — Day 4

Complete each word to finish the sentence. Fill in the gaps using the letters from the boxes.

Clive was a naughty sh...ee...p.

| ea | ee | ie | igh |

1. He liked films that gave him a fr........t.

2. "Let's sn........k out," said Clive.

3. The other sheep agr........d.

4. They left the f........ld and went to the cinema.

5. "Pl........se may we have some tickets?" they asked.

6. The man at the till could not bel........ve his eyes.

7. "Go to the first scr........n," he told them.

8. They had a fun n........t!

Today I scored [ ] out of 8.

Week 5 — Day 5

Read each sentence. Write the correct spelling of the word in bold.

Ffion had a magic **spewn**. ...spoon...

(1) It made the best **fude**. ....

(2) Ffion was cooking **stoo**. ....

(3) There was a loud **bewm**! ....

(4) She **knue** something was wrong. ....

(5) She couldn't **rescoo** her meal. ....

(6) It was thick like **glew**! ....

(7) "It can't be **tru**!" shouted Ffion. ....

(8) Ffion **throo** her spoon away. ....

Today I scored ☐ out of 8.

Year 2 Spelling — Summer Term

Week 6 — Day 1

1

sun

son

2

won

one

3

be

bee

4

blew

blue

5

see

sea

6

bear

bare

7

tale

tail

8

quiet

quite

Today I scored ____ out of 8.

Week 6 — Day 2

Add either '**y**', '**ie**' or '**igh**' to the words in bold to complete the sentences.

Zak is a sp....**y**.... .

(1) He is on a mission **ton**..........**t**.

(2) Zak **cr**..........**s** because he doesn't like the dark.

(3) Then, he has to **fl**.......... to a secret place.

(4) He lands on a **h**.......... building.

(5) Zak feels ill because he is **terrif**..........**d** of falling.

(6) Zak has to **f**..........**t** lots of baddies.

(7) But he is very **sh**.......... and runs away.

(8) This may not be the **r**..........**t** job for Zak!

Today I scored [ ] out of 8.

Year 2 Spelling — Summer Term

Week 6 — Day 3

Draw lines between the letters in each box to spell a word.
The first letter of the word is red.
Use the picture to help you.

c c l
i r e

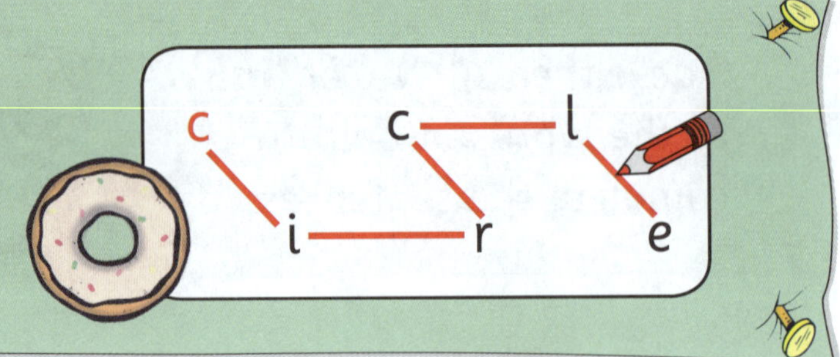

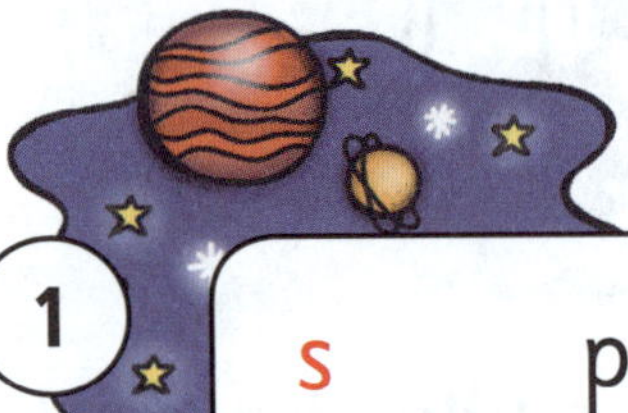

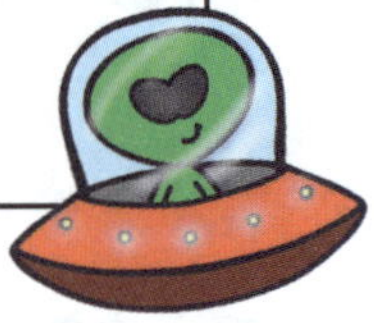

1

s p e
a c

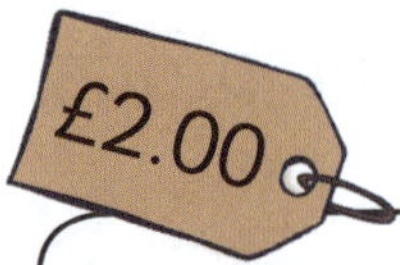

2

p i c
r e

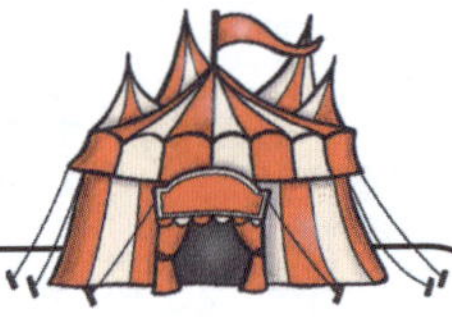

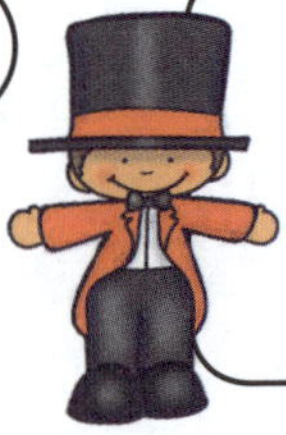

3

i r u
c c s

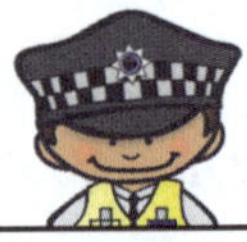

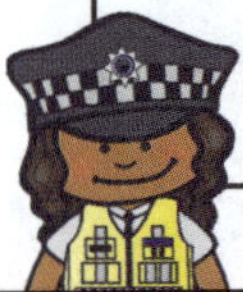

4

p o l
e c i

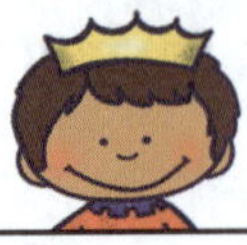

5

p i n
r c e

6

i n e
c m a

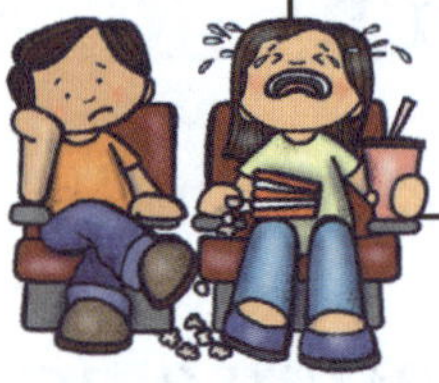

7

a p c
l a e

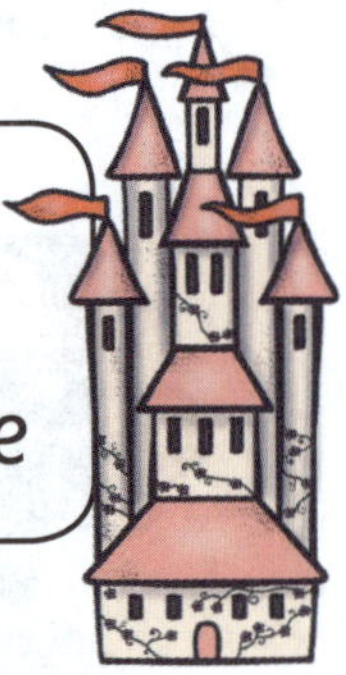

8

i c e
i c l

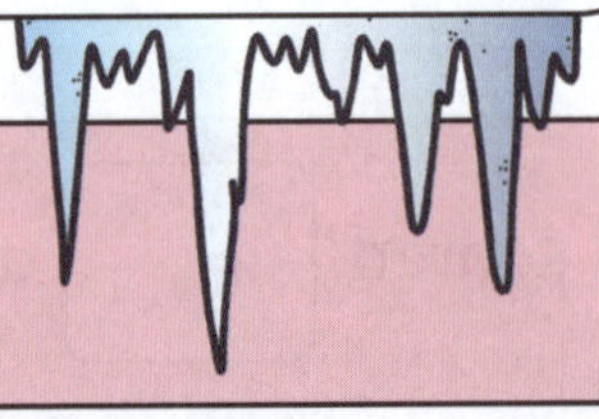

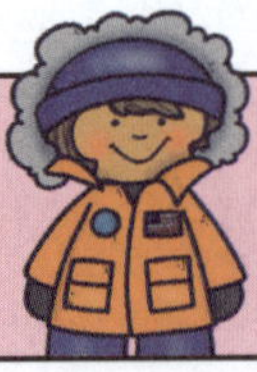

Today I scored ☐ out of 8.

Week 6 — Day 4

Use the sentences and pictures to help you fill in the missing letters in the boxes below.

A **st__m** is raging.

| s | t | o | r | m |

1 Rex **sn___s** loudly.

| s | n | | | s |

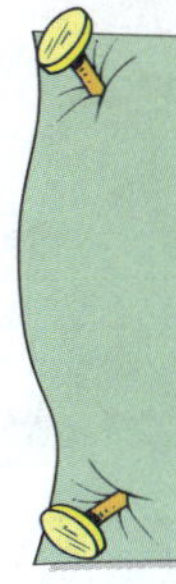

2 A rocket **l__nches** into the air.

| l | | n | c | h | e | s |

3 Jamal **dr__s** a picture.

| d | r | | s |

4 May is riding a **h__se**.

| h | | s | e |

5 The owl **squ__ks**.

| s | q | u | | k | s |

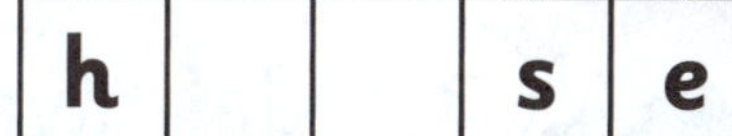

6 Tina is doing **ch___s**.

| c | h | | | s |

7 I **p__sed** the TV.

| p | | s | e | d |

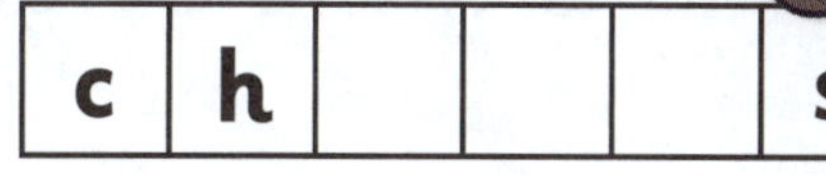

8 The caterpillar **cr__ls** on the leaf.

| c | r | | l | s |

Today I scored [ ] out of 8.

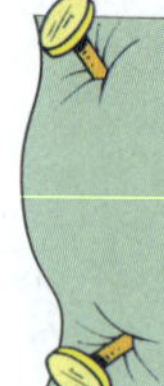

Week 6 — Day 5

The pictures and sentences below tell a story.
Write the correct spelling of the words in bold.

(1) Jeff is a **jiraffe**. ....

(2) He owns a pink **ggem**. ....

(3) Jeff lives in a **villadge**. ....

(4) Nearby there is a **brige**. ....

(5) This is where Gordon the **jiant** lives. ....

(6) Gordon wants to take the **dgewel**. ....

(7) He **chardges** at Jeff. ....

(8) Jeff **dojes** him! ....

Today I scored [ ] out of 8.

Week 7 — Day 1

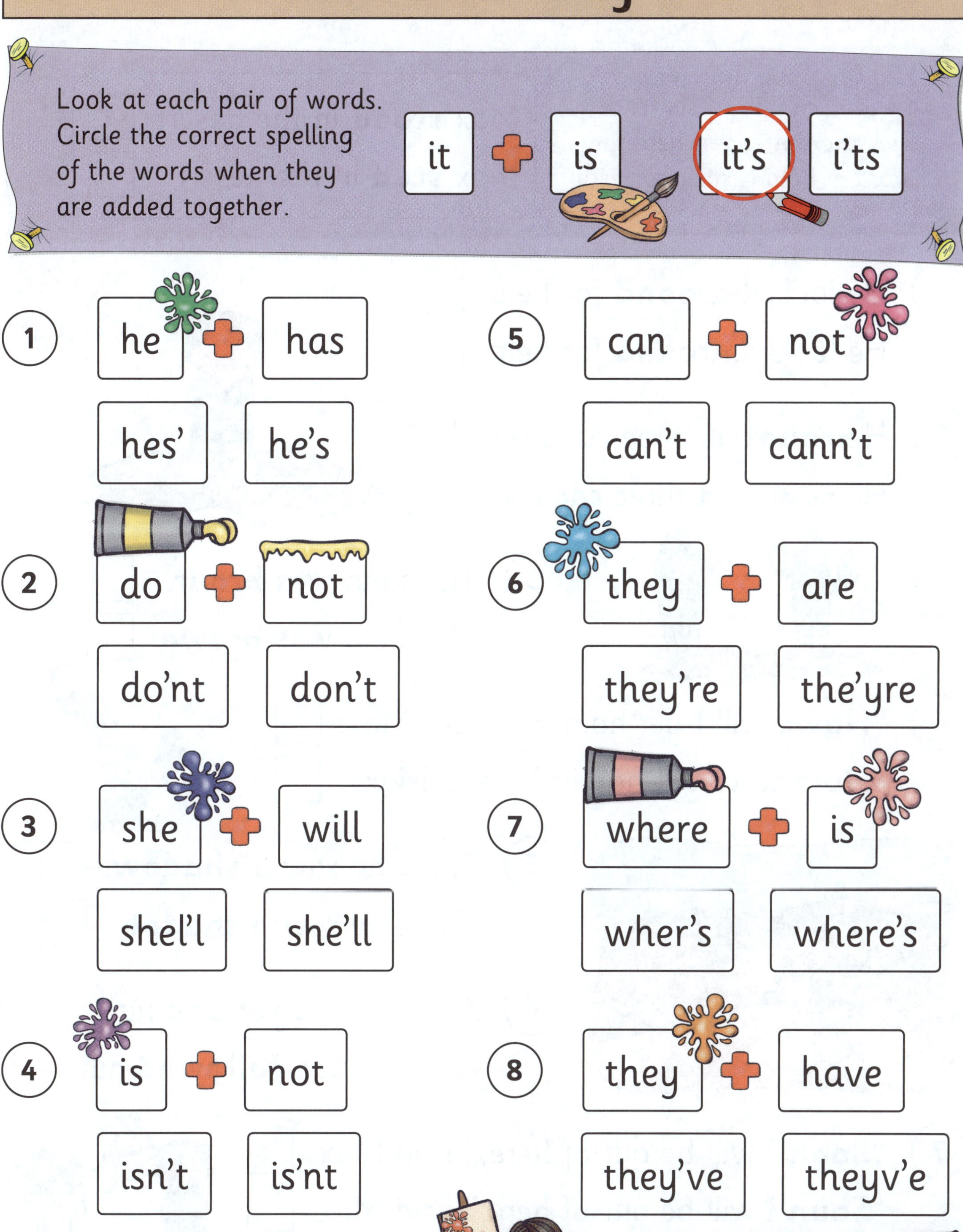

Today I scored [ ] out of 8.

Year 2 Spelling — Summer Term

Week 7 — Day 2

Read each pair of sentences. Tick the sentence where the word in bold is spelt correctly.

Max **stood** in the desert. ✔
Max **stud** in the desert. ☐

1) He looked **aroond** for help. ☐
He looked **around** for help. ☐

2) He **counted** three cactuses. ☐
He **cownted** three cactuses. ☐

3) The sand was **broun**. ☐
The sand was **brown**. ☐

4) "**Howe** will I get home?" asked Max. ☐
"**How** will I get home?" asked Max. ☐

5) Then, he saw a **shadow**. ☐
Then, he saw a **shadoo**. ☐

6) A camel had **folloed** him. ☐
A camel had **followed** him. ☐

7) "**Soon** I will be out of here," said Max. ☐
"**Soun** I will be out of here," said Max. ☐

Today I scored ☐ out of 7.

Week 7 — Day 3

Look at the pictures.
Complete each compound
word to finish the sentence.

Julia uses the sauce…**pan**… .

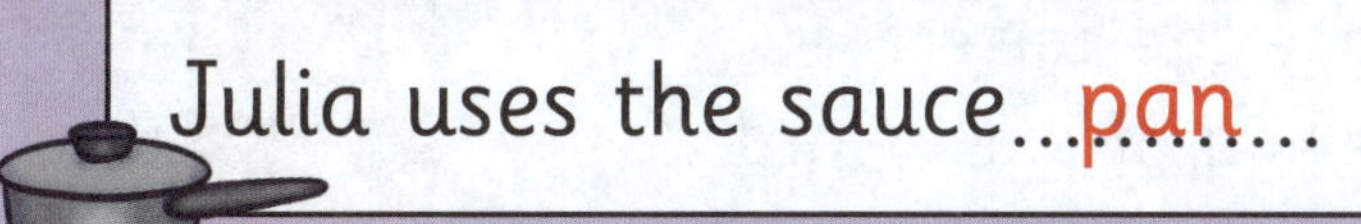

1 Fliss wants a pet jelly……………… !

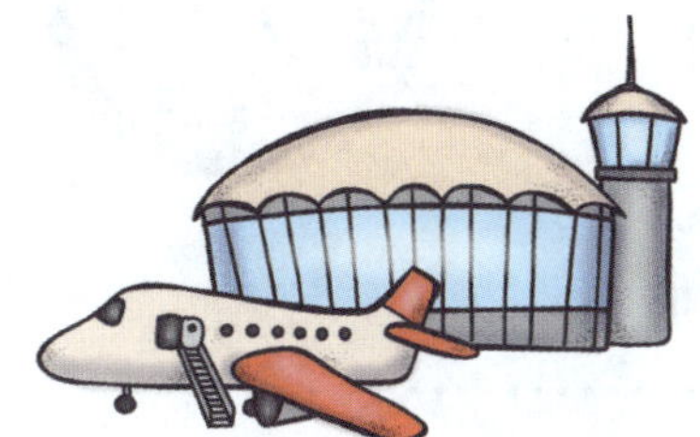

2 Mr Evans goes to the air……………… .

3 Helen had a hot……………… for lunch.

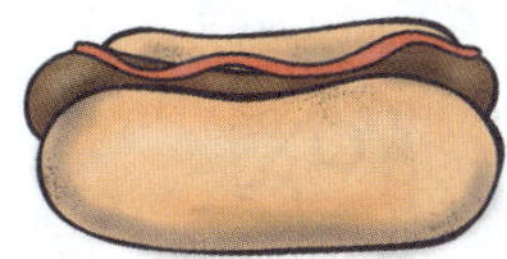

4 The scare……………… is in the field.

5 Grandma sits in an arm……………… .

6 Charles tidies his bed……………… .

7 Eugenia's tea……………… is blue and pink.

8 Harry lost his book……………… .

Today I scored ☐ out of 8.

   Year 2 Spelling — Summer Term

Week 7 — Day 4

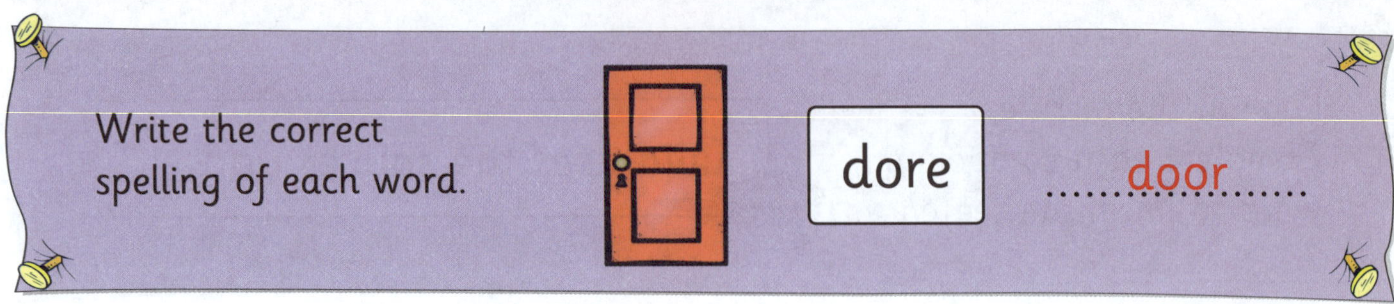

1 ohld ....

5 howr ....

2  harf ....

6 stayk ....

3 gowld 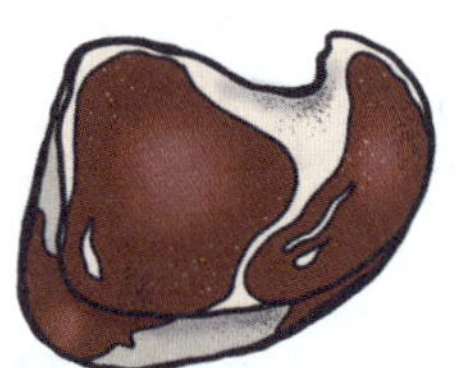 ....

7 shuger  ....

4 clohths ....

8  pairents ....

Today I scored ☐ out of 8.

Week 7 — Day 5

Read each sentence. Write the correct spelling of the word in bold.

"Can I **hav** a magic stone?" asked Mia. ....have....

1. The wizard did not **moove**. ....

2. "You must **leev**!" he thundered. ....

3. Mia was feeling **brayv**. ....

4. "I **deserv** a magic stone!" she shouted. ....

5. "You must **proov** it," said the wizard. ....

6. Mia had to **solv** a puzzle. ....

7. "I will **giv** you a stone," he said. ....

8. "But it is hidden in this **cayve**." ....

9. "A monster **livs** in there too." ....

Today I scored [   ] out of 9.

Year 2 Spelling — Summer Term

Week 8 — Day 1

Look at the pictures. Draw lines to match each word with the letters that are missing.

Today I scored [ ] out of 10.

Week 8 — Day 2

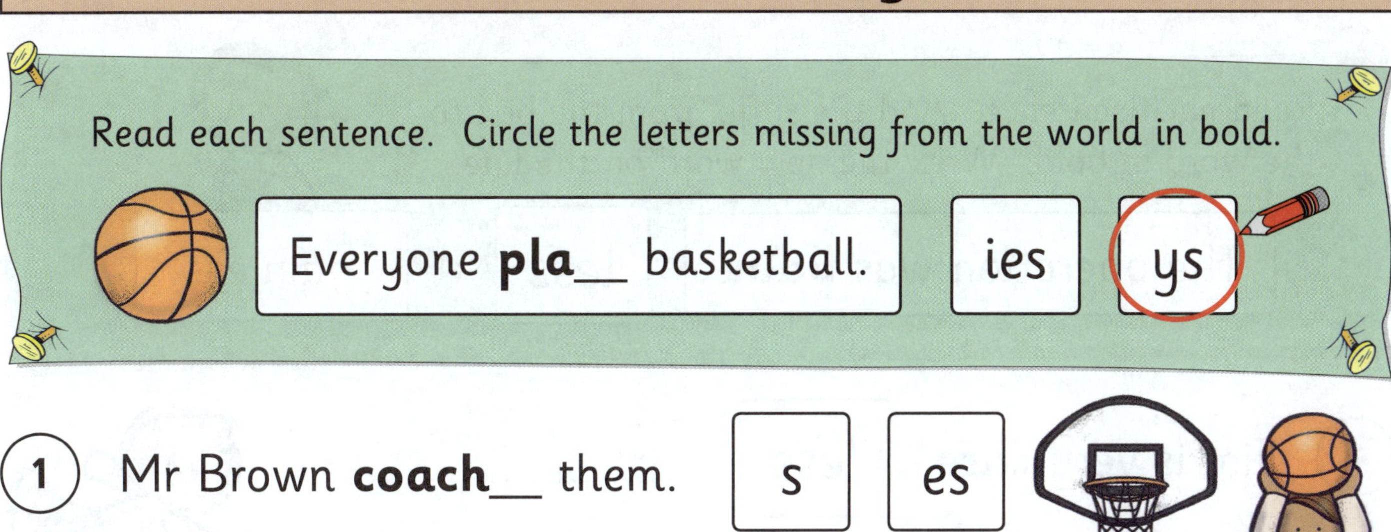

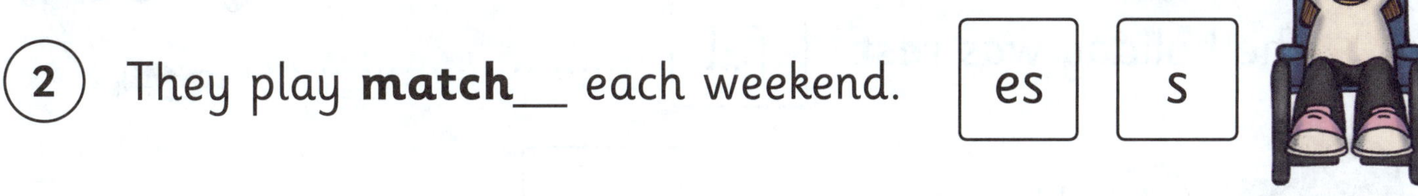

2 They play **match**__ each weekend.
es
s

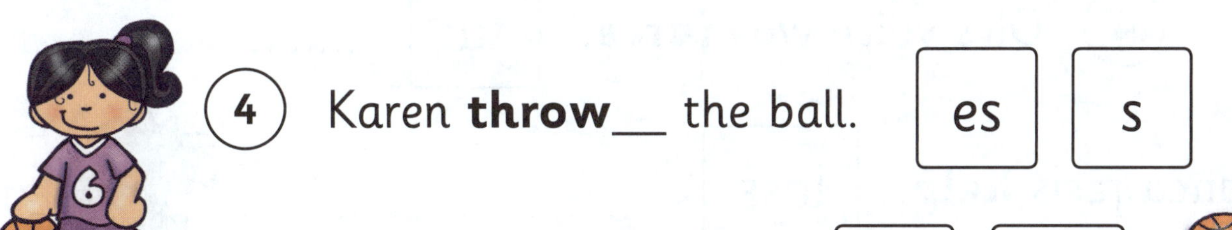

5 Jack **tr**__ to grab it.
ys
ies

6 Natalie **catch**__ the basketball.
es
s

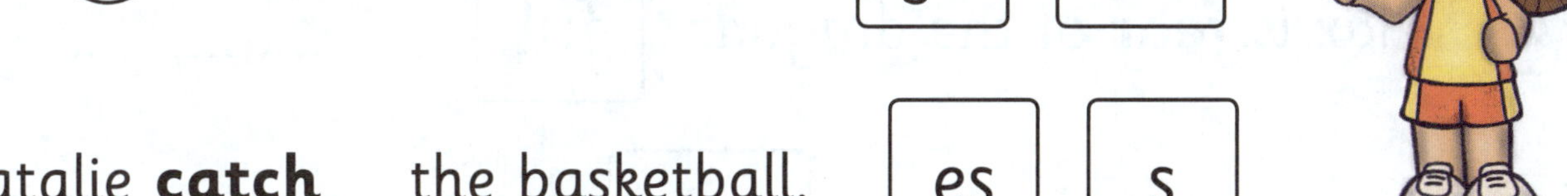

8 He **watch**__ as the girls score again.
s
es

   Year 2 Spelling — Summer Term

Week 8 — Day 3

Read each sentence. Add the suffix from the box to the word in bold. Write the new word on the line.

The operation was **pain**. | less | *painless*

1. Jim is very **care**. | less | ....

2. The holiday was **rest**. | ful | ....

3. Nuru is **speech**! | less | ....

4. Oli's voice was **force**. | ful | ....

5. Bianca feels **help**. | less | ....

6. Max is **fear** of the dragon. | ful | ....

7. Tidying is a **joy** task. | less | ....

8. My dog is very **play**. | ful | ....

9. I am **hope** we will win the game. | ful | ....

Today I scored ☐ out of 9.

Week 8 — Day 4

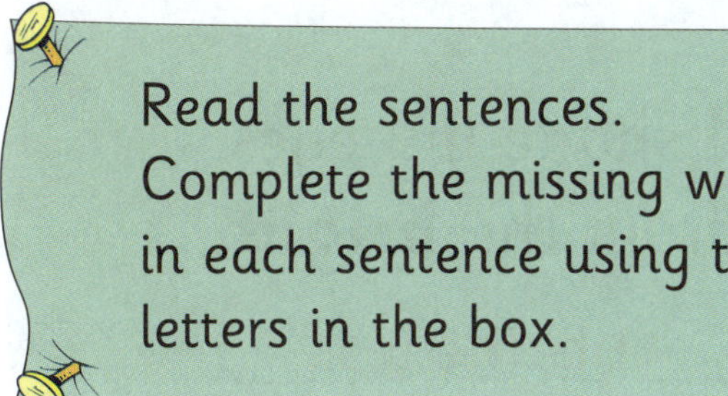

Read the sentences. Complete the missing word in each sentence using the letters in the box.

1. She has to **h**................... on tightly. `l o d`

2. She goes **e**................... week. `e r v y`

3. Sometimes she falls on the **f**................... . `o r o l`

4. But she always gets up **a**................... ! `g i a n`

5. Tess thinks climbing is **g**................... . `e a t r`

6. She is **p**................... good at it. `t t r y e`

7. Her **f**................... is proud of her. `t h a e r`

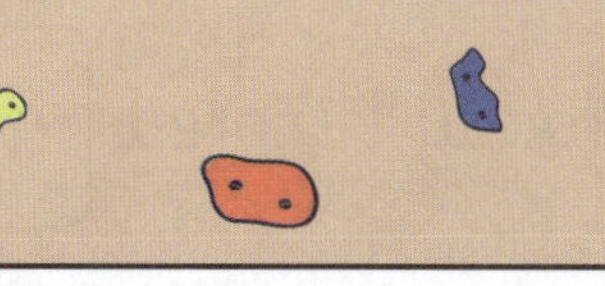

Today I scored [ ] out of 7.

Week 8 — Day 5

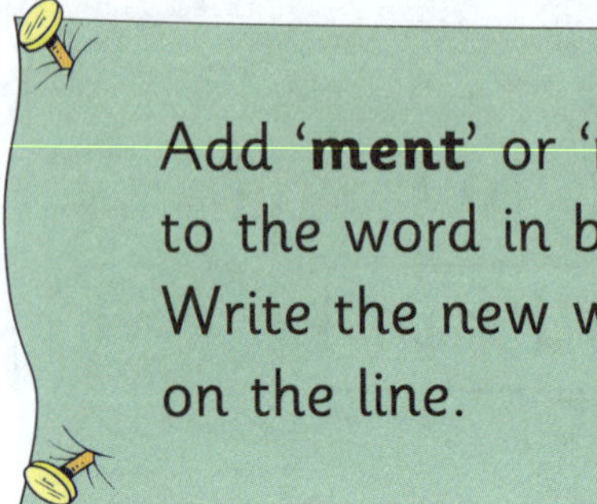

Add 'ment' or 'ness' to the word in bold. Write the new word on the line.

I shade my eyes from the **bright**.

.... brightness ....

1 A sudden **move** surprised me. ....

2 Jared has a mild **ill**. ....

3 Milo's **treat** is going well. ....

4 Lesley's **clever** is amazing! ....

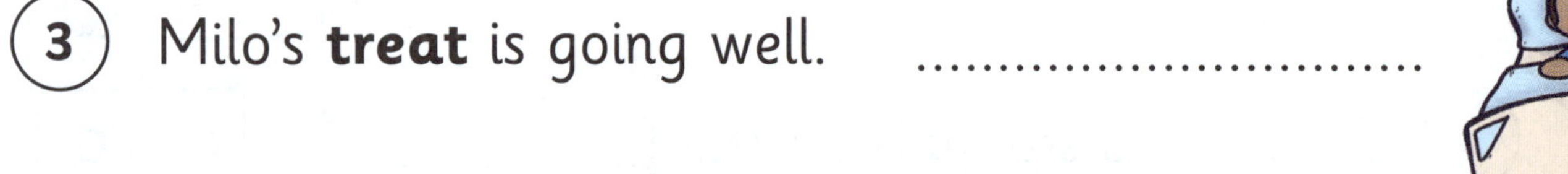

5 Wojtek won't stop his **silly**. ....

6 They make the **pay**. ....

7 Kim suffers from **shy**. ....

8 I've never seen such **messy**! ....

9 We had an **argue** about cheese. ....

Today I scored ☐ out of 9.

Week 9 — Day 1

Put a ✔ in the box if the word in bold is spelt correctly.
Put a ✘ if the word in bold is not spelt correctly.

The **dayly** routine of a superhero is busy. ✘

1. **Firstly**, you have to leap out of bed. ☐

2. You need to eat breakfast **quicklly**. ☐

3. There's no time to **lazily** chew your toast! ☐

4. Then, you have to dress **smarttly**. ☐

5. **Finally**, it's time to get to work. ☐

6. You must react **speedily** to everything. ☐

7. You should always be helpful and **friendily**. ☐

8. It's hard work fighting crime **constantly**! ☐

9. **Happyly**, everyone thanks you for your hard work. ☐

Today I scored ☐ out of 9.

Week 9 — Day 2

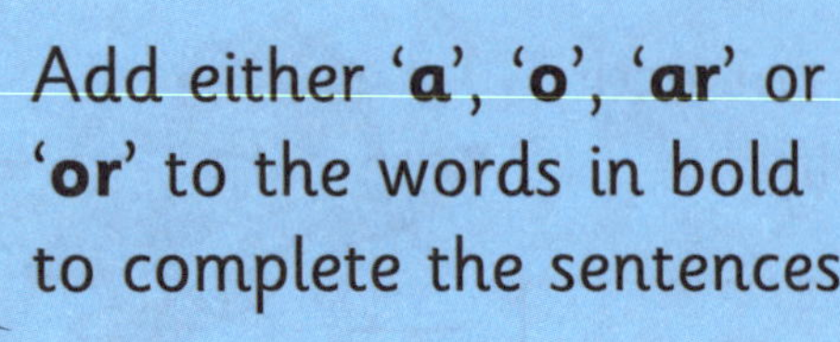

Add either 'a', 'o', 'ar' or 'or' to the words in bold to complete the sentences.

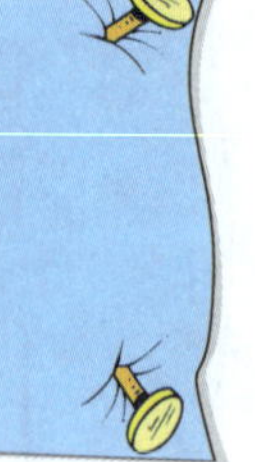

I feel too **w** ar **m**.

1. Tabitha **w.......nts** a pony for her birthday.

2. The jelly is very **w.......bbly**.

3. Gina walks **tow.......ds** the dog.

4. The cake is **w.......nderful**.

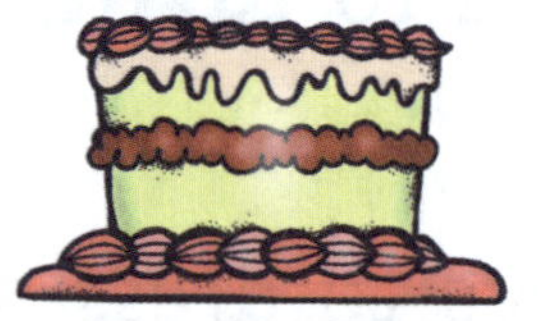

5. "This is the **w.......st** day ever!" shouted Sam.

6. Lara ate an enormous **qu.......ntity** of sweets.

7. The witch was **rew.......ded** for saving a fairy.

8. The ring is **w.......th** a lot of money.

9. The **qu.......lity** of Kwame's art is amazing.

Today I scored ☐ out of 9.

Week 9 — Day 3

Look at the pictures.
Fill in the missing letters
to correctly spell the word.

a n n ...o... ...y... e d

1.  b l

2. .... s t e r 

3. 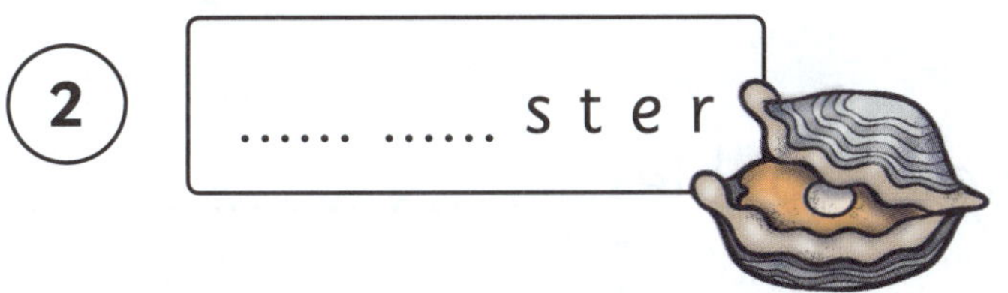 p .... n t

4. j o ..... f ..... l 

5.  t o .... e t

6. 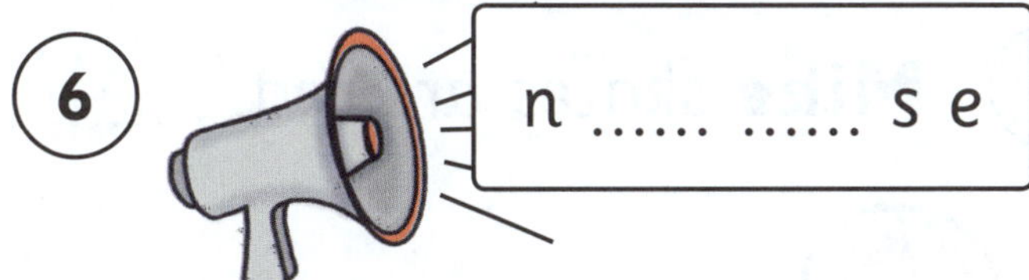 n .... s e

7. v .... a g e 

8. c ..... w b .... 

9. p .... s o ..... 

10. d e ..... t ..... o ..... 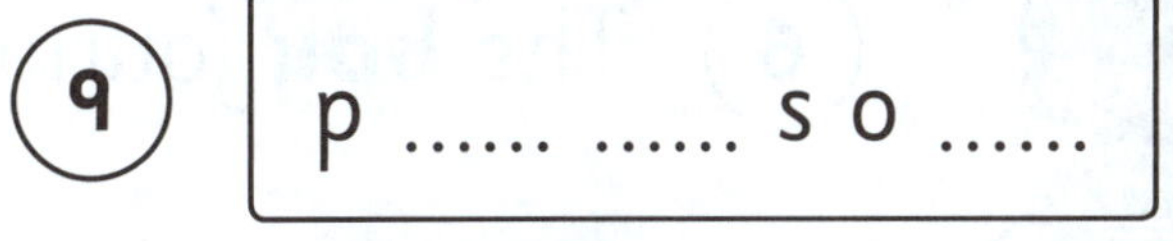

Today I scored ☐ out of 10.

Year 2 Spelling — Summer Term

Week 9 — Day 4

Rewrite the words in bold adding an apostrophe and 's'.

the **bike** wheel ....bike's..........

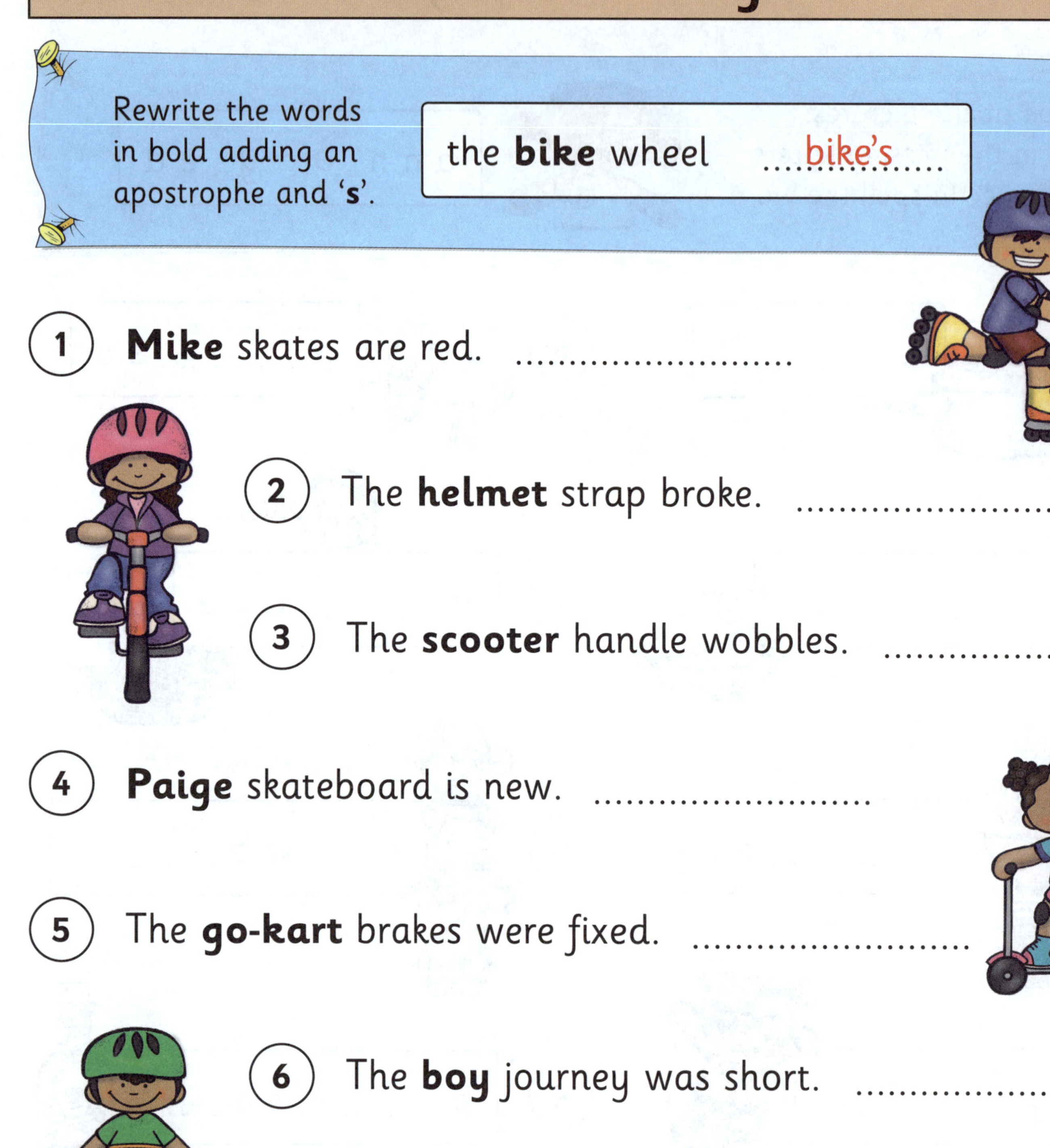

1. **Mike** skates are red. ....

2. The **helmet** strap broke. ....

3. The **scooter** handle wobbles. ....

4. **Paige** skateboard is new. ....

5. The **go-kart** brakes were fixed. ....

6. The **boy** journey was short. ....

7. **James** shoes were muddy. ....

8. The **class** games are fun to play. ....

Today I scored [ ] out of 8.

Week 9 — Day 5

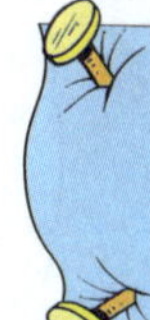

Write the correct spelling of each word in bold to complete the crossword.

Down

2) "Come **hear**," Tamsin said.

5) Em ties a **not** in the rope.

6) I like to **role** down hills.

8) They **stair** at him in shock.

9) Guy's favourite colour is **read**.

10) Ling **nose** my sister.

Across

1) "It's lovely to **meat** you," he said.

3) The **night** has shiny armour.

4) This **flour** has beautiful petals.

7) We ate snacks during our **brake**.

Today I scored ☐ out of 10.

Year 2 Spelling — Summer Term

Week 10 — Day 1

Read each sentence. Circle the word in bold if it is spelt correctly. <u>Underline</u> it if it is **not** spelt correctly.

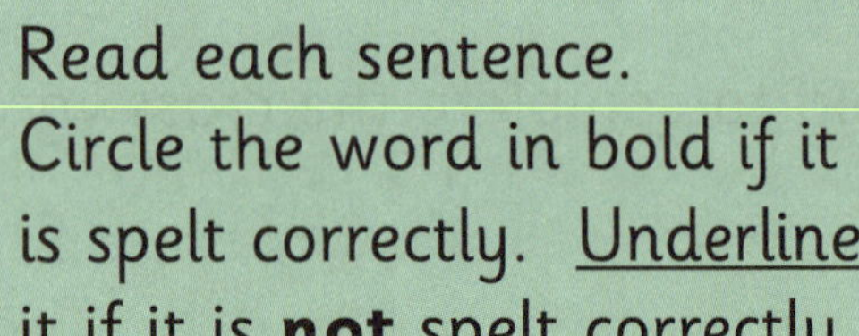

1. There is **nothing** in the jar. 

2. I went shopping the **outher** day.

3. On **Munday**, Pete goes swimming.

4. A friendly **woman** smiles at me.

5. The birds fly **abov** our heads. 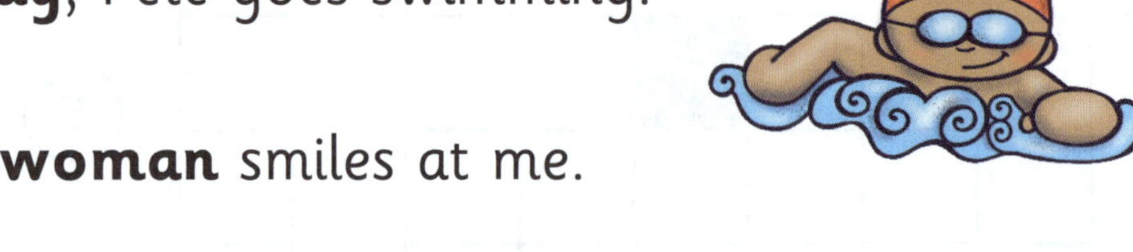

6. My grandparents **come** for lunch.

7. Sharon's birthday is next **munth**.

8. The **ovn** burns everything.

9. Fran **discovered** some treasure.

10. Our chickens laid a **duzen** eggs. 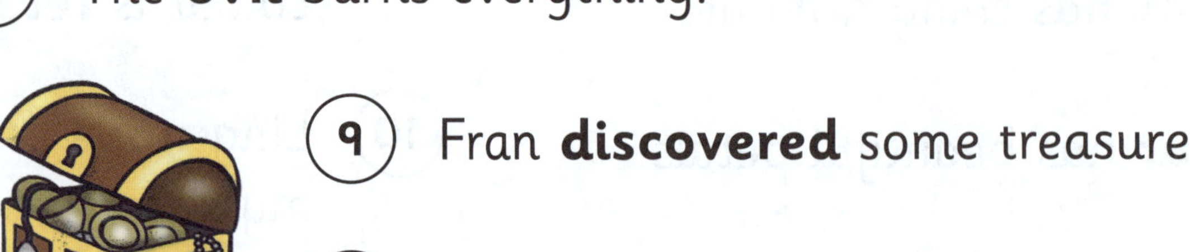

Today I scored ☐ out of 10.

Week 10 — Day 2

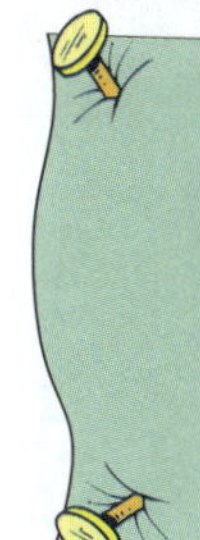

Read each sentence. Circle the letters missing from the world in bold.

Kaia is watching the **televi__**. | tion | **sion** (circled)

1. There is a **fic__al** show on. | tion | sion |

2. It's about an **inva__** of dogs. | tion | sion |

3. Their **ambi__** is to take over the world. | tion | sion |

4. There are lots of **explo__s**. | tion | sion |

5. One of the dogs loses his **vi__**. | tion | sion |

6. He might need an **opera__**. | tion | sion |

7. But the vet rubs in some **lo__** and the dog is cured! | tion | sion |

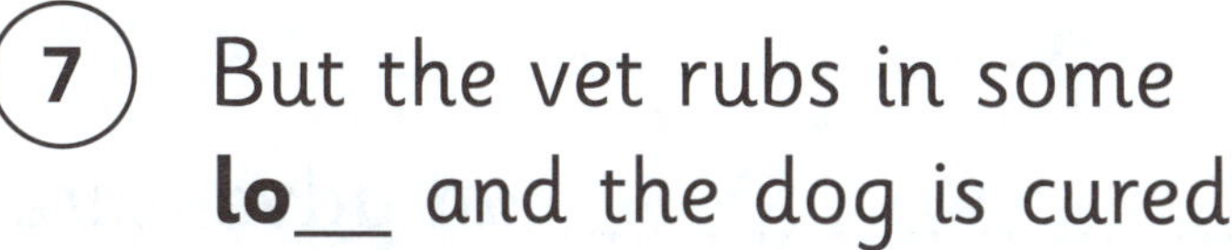

8. It is a very **emo__al** show. | tion | sion |

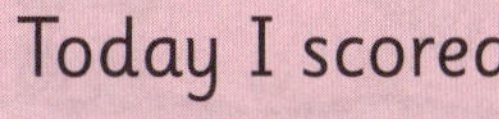

Today I scored [ ] out of 8.

Year 2 Spelling — Summer Term

Week 10 — Day 3

Add the suffix to the word in bold. Write the new word on the line.

Jay is a forest [**explore** + er] ...explorer... .

1. Will loves [**hike** + ing] ....

2. Hetty [**chat** + ed] .... to Stu.

3. Flo is [**worry** + ed] .... about falling.

4. Duong is [**brave** + er] .... than Alice.

5. Kat [**carry** + ed] .... some leaves.

6. Nick is [**balance** + ing] .... on a log.

7. This is the [**pretty** + est] .... flower.

8. Felix is [**plan** + ing] .... an adventure.

9. The tree is [**big** + er] .... than Diane.

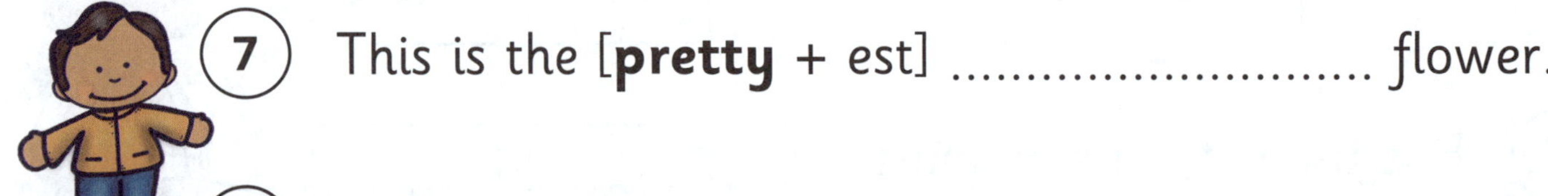

Today I scored [ ] out of 9.

Week 10 — Day 4

Look at the pictures.
Write the correct
spelling of each word.

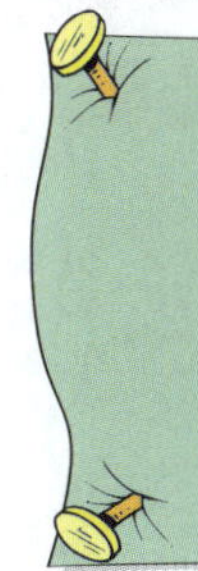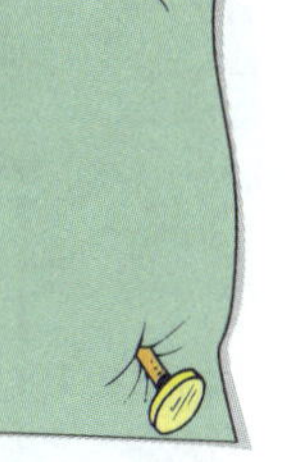

kandle

candle

1  duc
....

6  bounsy
....

2 pensil 
....

7 loket 
....

3  kamera
....

8  cettle
....

4 cacktus 
....

9 symbals 
....

5  kuddle
....

10  carate
....

Today I scored ☐ out of 10. 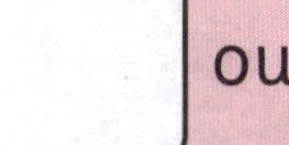

Week 10 — Day 5

Read each sentence. Write the correct spelling of the word in bold.

The mice **squeek**. ....*squeak*........

1 Yola has **threa** pet kittens. ....

2 They **compeet** in cat contests. ....

3 Yola **dremes** of them winning. ....

4 She **teeches** her kittens tricks. ....

5 Everyone **agreas** the kittens are skilled. ....

6 They are very **swete** to look at. ....

7 But there's a **reeson** they lose. ....

8 Yola's kittens are **chekey**! ....

9 Judges think **theas** kittens are naughty. ....

Today I scored ☐ out of 9.

Week 11 — Day 1

1 One **afternewn** / **afternoon** , we went to pick some.

2 They gave us **wuden** / **wooden** baskets to put them in.

3 I wanted to pick a **thousand** / **thowsand** strawberries.

4 My cousin spotted a **narro** / **narrow** path.

5 Then, he **found** / **fownd** the biggest strawberry ever!

6 It was **enormous** / **enormuss** .

7 It wouldn't fit **indaws** / **indoors** .

8 A **crowd** / **croud** of people came to see it.

9 My cousin was very **proud** / **prowd** .

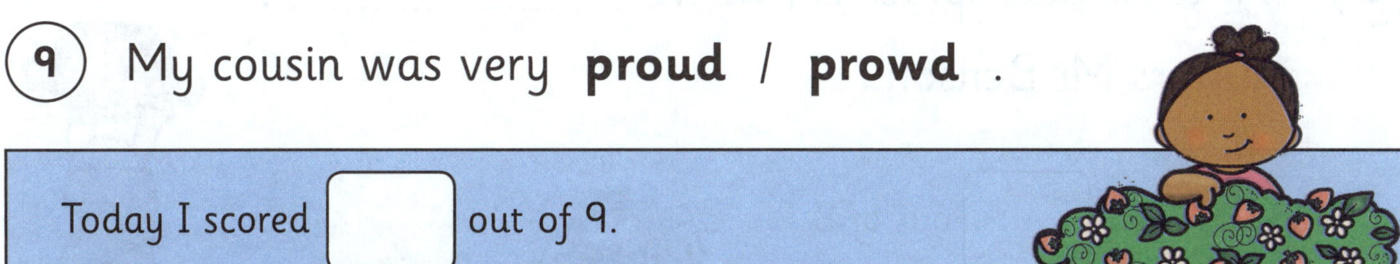

Today I scored ☐ out of 9.

   Year 2 Spelling — Summer Term

Week 11 — Day 2

Add the suffix '**less**' to the word in bold. Write the new word on the line.

Mr Benson's shop is [**end**] ......*endless*...... .

1 He has [**count**] .... things in there.

2 He is [**hope**] .... at sorting it out.

3 "All this stuff is [**worth**] .... !" says Sophie.

4 "It's [**price**] .... ," replies Mr Benson.

5 "No, it's [**use**] .... !" argues Sophie.

6 "That piano is [**tune**] ...."

7 "It's why the till is [**penny**] .... ," she shouts.

8 "At least that spider is [**harm**] .... ,"
mutters Mr Benson.

Today I scored [ ] out of 8.

Week 11 — Day 3

Use the sentences and pictures to help you fill in the missing letters in the boxes below.

The stars are **br__t**.

b	r	i	g	h	t

1 Ismail made some **p__s**.

p			s

2 The **sk__** is dark at night.

s	k	

3 Jacqui **t__s** her shoelaces.

t			s

4 Those **t__ts** are stripy.

t				t	s

5 Pippa makes a **fr__d** egg.

f	r			d

6 Jesse likes the **p__thon**.

p		t	h	o	n

7 Romie **s__ed** tiredly.

s			e	d

Today I scored [ ] out of 7.

Week 11 — Day 4

Read each sentence, then circle the word that is spelt incorrectly. Write the correct spelling on the line.

An (orthor) is writing a book. ....*author*...........

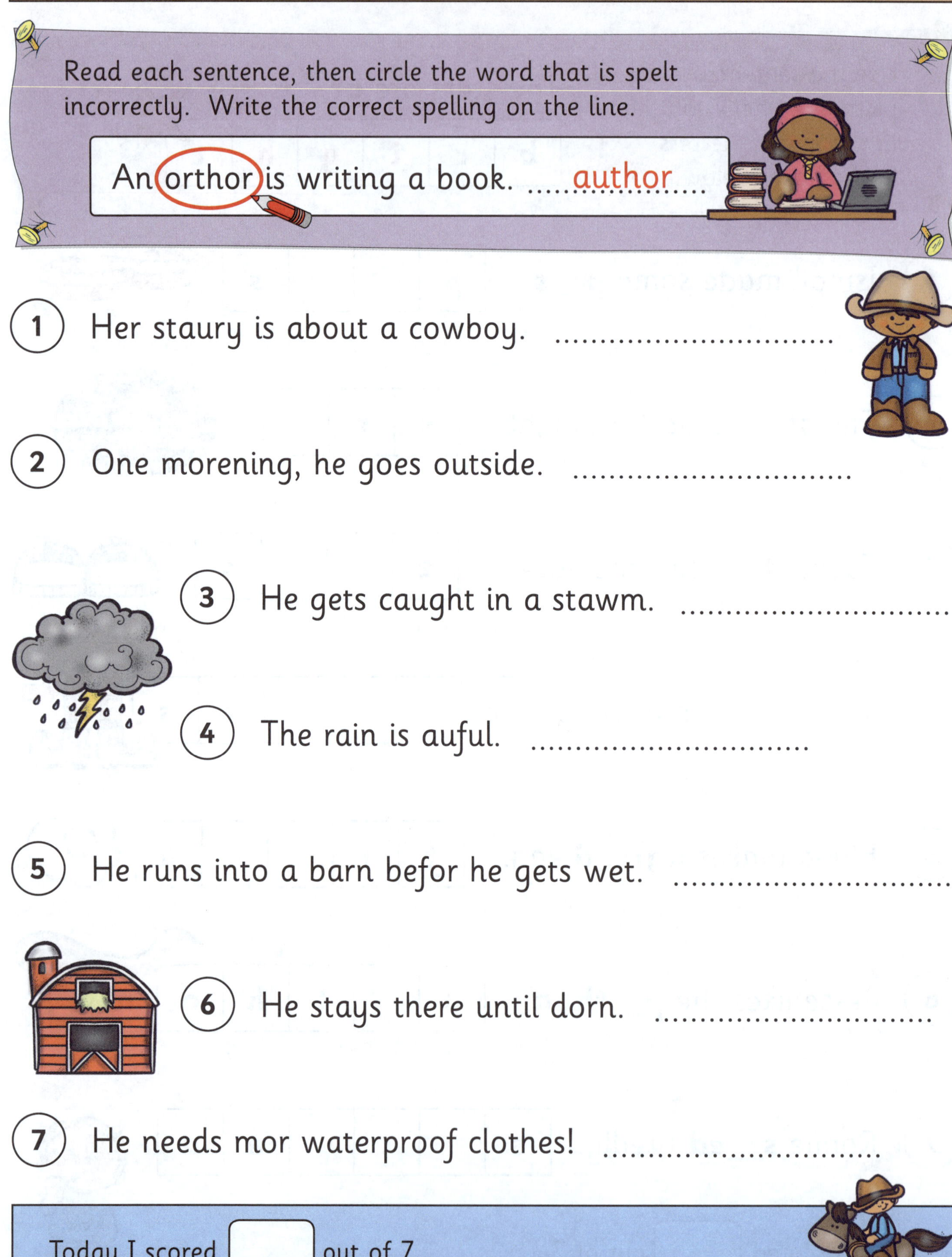

1 Her staury is about a cowboy. ....

2 One morening, he goes outside. ....

3 He gets caught in a stawm. ....

4 The rain is auful. ....

5 He runs into a barn befor he gets wet. ....

6 He stays there until dorn. ....

7 He needs mor waterproof clothes! ....

Today I scored [ ] out of 7.

Week 11 — Day 5

(1) Where is the **rise**?

....

(2) Bella needs to buy **selery**.

....

(3) Those oranges look **juisy**.

....

(4) Are these chillies **spisie**?

....

(5) Gemma couldn't **deside** what to buy.

....

(6) I can't find the **medisine**!

....

Today I scored ☐ out of 6.

Week 12 — Day 1

Add an apostrophe so that the word in bold is spelt correctly.

W e ' v e made biscuits.

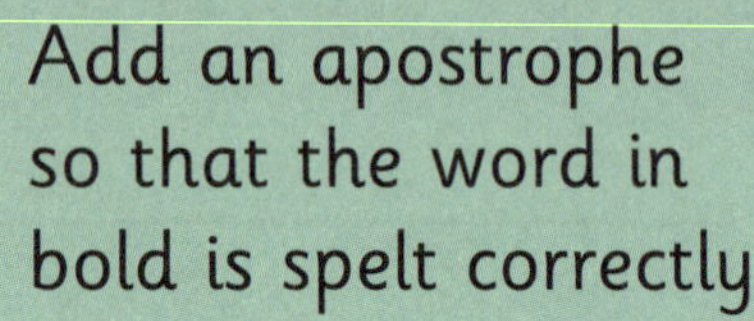

(1) **S o n i a s** cake looks amazing.

(2) **S h e s** iced it beautifully.

(3) The **b a k e r s** son made cupcakes.

(4) **H e l l** decorate them later on.

(5) **I v e** made chocolate chip cookies.

(6) **Y o u r e** all great at baking.

(7) I **h a v e n t** tried those tarts yet.

(8) **J e s s s** brownies look yummy.

(9) I **w o n t** have one — I am too full!

Today I scored [ ] out of 9.

Week 12 — Day 2

Add either '**tion**' or '**sion**' to the words in bold to complete the sentences.

I like practising **subtrac** tion .

1. The **mo**............ of the boat made me ill.

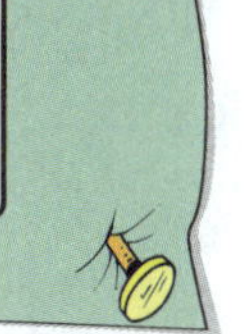

2. The **loca**............ of the play is a city.

3. The lord and lady live in a **man**............ .

4. **Ten**............ is building at the contest.

5. Laila's **ver**............ of the story is very funny.

6. My **posi**............ in hockey is goalkeeper.

7. The nurse gives Jamie an **injec**............ .

8. There was a **colli**............ in the car park.

9. Juan is waiting at the train **sta**............ .

Today I scored [ ] out of 9.

Year 2 Spelling — Summer Term

Week 12 — Day 3

Use the words in the boxes to complete the sentences below. Add '**ly**' to each word. Each word should only be used once.

| careful |

Helen approached the dragon ....*carefully*.......... .

| playful | | loud | | sudden | | tight | | angry | | quiet |

1. She tiptoed .... so he wouldn't hear her.

2. But ...., she stepped on a twig.

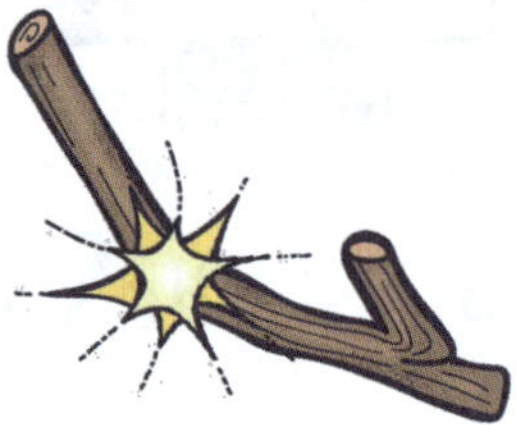

3. It snapped .... with a crack.

4. "Who's there?" shouted the dragon ....

5. "Surprise!" laughed Helen ....

6. The dragon hugged his friend Helen ....

Today I scored [ ] out of 6.

Week 12 — Day 4

Add the correct suffix to the word in bold. Write the new word on the line. Choose from '**ment**', '**ful**' or '**ness**'.

The runner's **fit** is amazing.

.........fitness.........

(**1**) Bats fly through the **dark**. ....

(**2**) My sister is **use** in the kitchen. ....

(**3**) The **state** didn't make sense. ....

(**4**) Fatima is a **success** artist. ....

(**5**) My biggest **weak** is chocolate. ....

(**6**) They had a big **disagree**. ....

(**7**) I have a doctor's **appoint**. ....

(**8**) This ice cream is **delight**. ....

(**9**) Spinning fast can cause **dizzy**. ....

Today I scored [ ] out of 9.

Year 2 Spelling — Summer Term

Week 12 — Day 5

Read each sentence, then circle the word that is spelt incorrectly. Write the correct spelling on the line.

The (chilldren) were playing in the woods. ...children...

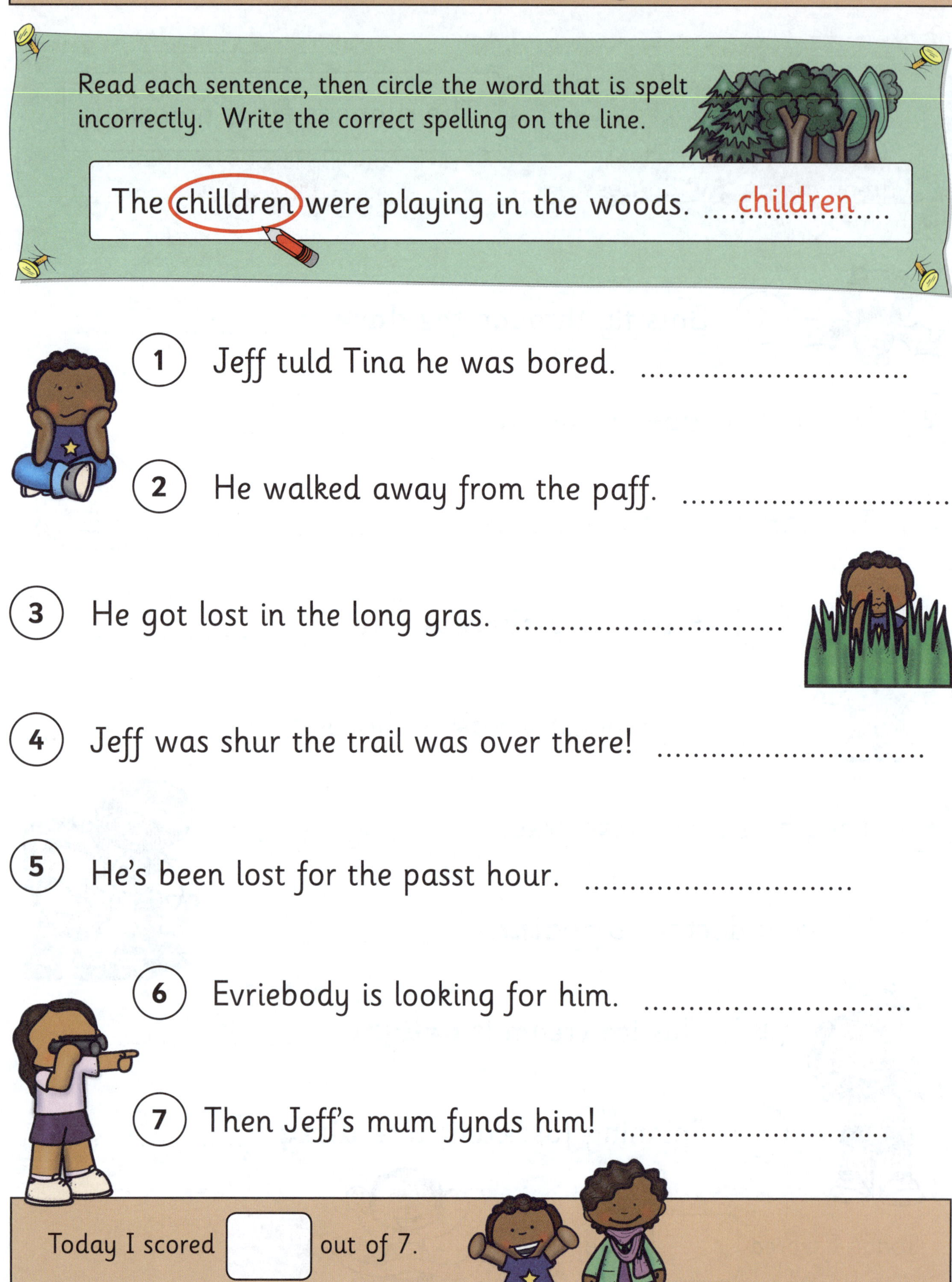

1. Jeff tuld Tina he was bored. ....

2. He walked away from the paff. ....

3. He got lost in the long gras. ....

4. Jeff was shur the trail was over there! ....

5. He's been lost for the passt hour. ....

6. Evriebody is looking for him. ....

7. Then Jeff's mum fynds him! ....

Today I scored [ ] out of 7.

Answers

Week 1 — Day 1

1. ✔
2. ✗
3. ✔
4. ✔
5. ✗
6. ✗
7. ✗
8. ✔

Week 1 — Day 2

1. face
2. **k**ing
3. dance
4. sna**ck**
5. **c**ycle
6. li**ck**
7. **c**astle
8. prin**c**ess

Week 1 — Day 3

1. Mobo opens the **parcel**.
2. The **pupil** raises her hand.
3. The **eagle** flaps its wings.
4. A cheetah is a wild **animal**.
5. Zosia **travels** all over the world.
6. **Camels** live in the desert.
7. Joe wants to be a **jungle** explorer.
8. Imani finds a rare **fossil**.

Week 1 — Day 4

1. floated
2. copying
3. spotty
4. flipper
5. stripiest
6. diver
7. swimming
8. studied

Week 1 — Day 5

1. foxes
2. branches
3. crunches
4. berries
5. bushes
6. babies
7. flies

Week 2 — Day 1

1. gloves
2. mother
3. funny
4. shove
5. honey
6. brother
7. shovel

Week 2 — Day 2

1. ✗
2. ✔
3. ✗
4. ✔
5. ✔
6. ✗
7. ✗
8. ✔

Week 2 — Day 3

1. She is small and colourful.
2. She is also a parrot!
3. Although Polly is quite old, she can still do a lot.
4. She can perform all sorts of amazing tricks.
5. She talks and squawks loudly.
6. She can draw pictures with chalk.
7. She walks on her pointy claws.
8. Polly can even play football.

Week 2 — Day 4

1. wand
2. warn
3. wash
4. squat
5. swan
6. quarter
7. watch
8. quarrel

Week 2 — Day 5

1. **w**orm
2. world
3. s**w**arm
4. a**w**ard
5. **w**armth
6. **w**arthog
7. **war**drobe
8. w**or**ship

Week 3 — Day 1

1. letter
2. twirl
3. church
4. turtle
5. chirp
6. purse
7. first
8. tiger
9. anger
10. purple

Week 3 — Day 2

1. The **coldness** makes me shiver.
2. Sid cannot shake his **tiredness**.
3. The drink has an odd **bitterness**.
4. The **quietness** is broken by a squawk.
5. Zuko's **fluffiness** is well-known.
6. We love his **friendliness**.
7. I've never felt such **happiness**.
8. The **roughness** of the rock hurts my hand.
9. His **sadness** lifted when he saw her.

Week 3 — Day 3

1. Cynthia found a shiny c**oi**n.
2. My dad has a l**oy**al dog called Otis.
3. There was a c**oi**l of rope on the floor.
4. Bad weather sp**oi**led the barbecue.
5. "Stop ann**oy**ing your sister," said Mum.
6. The r**oy**al family live in an enormous castle.
7. Abeni has a lovely singing v**oi**ce.
8. Sasha's pet tort**oi**se can surf.

Week 3 — Day 4

1. agreement
2. refreshment
3. punishment
4. equipment
5. excitement
6. amusement
7. pavement
8. disappointment

Week 3 — Day 5

1. busy
2. many
3. water
4. friends
5. called
6. asked
7. looked
8. class
9. one

Week 4 — Day 1

1.	yes	5.	no
2.	no	6.	no
3.	yes	7.	yes
4.	no	8.	no

Week 4 — Day 2

1. He is having a picnic at his **mum's** house.
2. His **classmates** come.
3. **Taraji's** dad brings lemonade.
4. Harvey has made some **pasties**.
5. **Kyle's** biscuits are yummy.
6. That juice is **Edward's**.
7. Jasmine likes the **sandwiches**.
8. Granddad lights the **candles**.

Week 4 — Day 3

1.	✔	6.	✔
2.	✘	7.	✘
3.	✘	8.	✔
4.	✘	9.	✔
5.	✔	10.	✘

Week 4 — Day 4

1.	shopper	6.	dropped
2.	reddest	7.	hottest
3.	pouring	8.	mixed
4.	chopping	9.	stirred
5.	toaster	10.	sweetest

Week 4 — Day 5

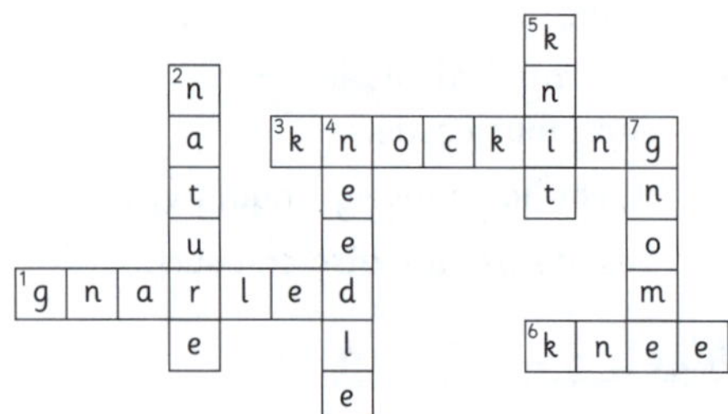

Week 5 — Day 1

1.	measure	5.	division
2.	leisure	6.	occasion
3.	casual	7.	inclusion
4.	confusion	8.	unusual

Week 5 — Day 2

1. "We must land **urgently**!" said the Captain.
2. They crashed **heavily** on the planet.
3. It was **nearly** a disaster.
4. **Luckily**, no one was hurt.
5. "Maybe we will find help," the Captain suggested **hopefully.**
6. **Eventually**, they found some aliens.
7. The aliens were **certainly** helpful.
8. They got the astronauts home **safely**!

Week 5 — Day 3

1. fiction
2. potion
3. eruption
4. emotion
5. addition
6. question
7. donation

Week 5 — Day 4

1. He liked films that gave him a fr**igh**t.
2. "Let's sn**ea**k out," said Clive.
3. The other sh**ee**p agreed.
4. They left the f**ie**ld and went to the cinema.
5. "Pl**ea**se may we have some tickets?" they asked.
6. The man at the till could not bel**ie**ve his eyes.
7. "Go to the first scr**ee**n," he told them.
8. They had a fun n**igh**t!

Week 5 — Day 5

1. food
2. stew
3. boom
4. knew
5. rescue
6. glue
7. true
8. threw

Week 6 — Day 1

1.	sun	5.	sea
2.	won	6.	bear
3.	bee	7.	tail
4.	blew	8.	quiet

Week 6 — Day 2

1. He is on a mission ton**igh**t.
2. Zak cr**ies** because he doesn't like the dark.
3. Then, he has to fl**y** to a secret place.
4. He lands on a h**igh** building.
5. Zak feels ill because he is terrif**ied** of falling.
6. Zak has to f**igh**t lots of baddies.
7. But he is very sh**y** and runs away.
8. This may not be the r**igh**t job for Zak!

Week 6 — Day 3

1. 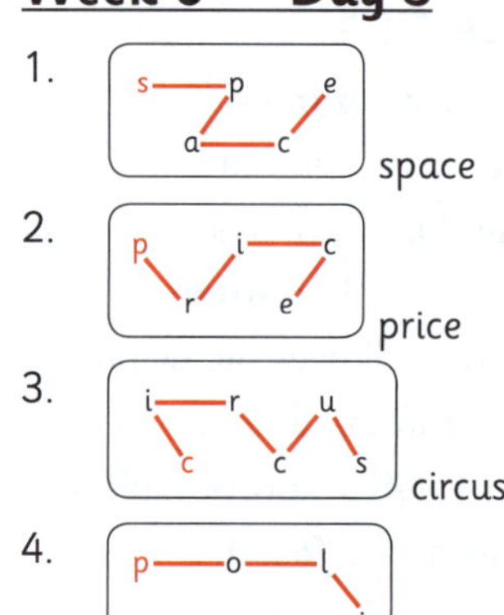 space

2. price

3. circus

4. 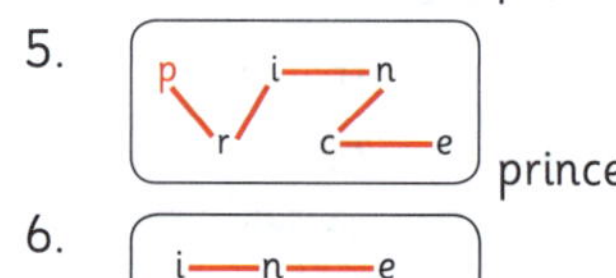 police

5. prince

6. 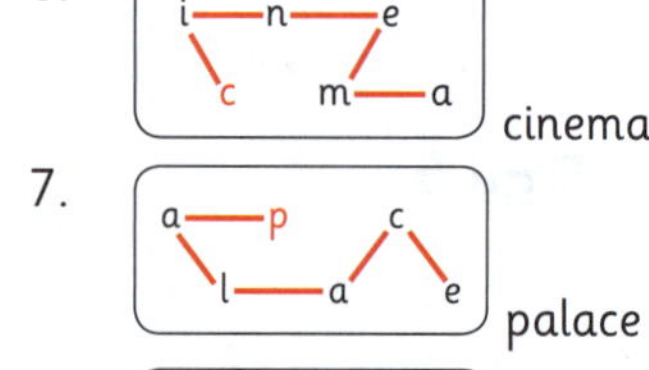 cinema

7. palace

8. 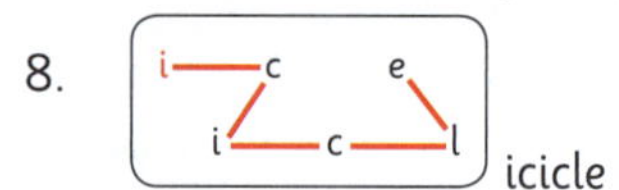 icicle

Week 6 — Day 4

1.	sn**ore**s	5.	squ**aw**ks
2.	l**au**nches	6.	ch**ore**s
3.	dr**aw**s	7.	p**au**sed
4.	h**or**se	8.	cr**aw**ls

Week 6 — Day 5

1.	giraffe	5.	giant
2.	gem	6.	jewel
3.	village	7.	charges
4.	bridge	8.	dodges

Answers

Week 7 — Day 1

1. he's	5. can't
2. don't	6. they're
3. she'll	7. where's
4. isn't	8. they've

Week 7 — Day 2

1. He looked **around** for help.
2. He **counted** three cactuses.
3. The sand was **brown**.
4. "**How** will I get home?" asked Max.
5. Then, he saw a **shadow**.
6. A camel had **followed** him.
7. "**Soon** I will be out of here," said Max.

Week 7 — Day 3

1. Fliss wants a pet jelly**fish**.
2. Mr Evans goes to the air**port**.
3. Helen had a hot**dog** for lunch.
4. The scare**crow** is in the field.
5. Grandma sits in an arm**chair**.
6. Charles tidies his bed**room**.
7. Eugenia's tea**pot** is blue and pink.
8. Harry lost his book**mark**.

Week 7 — Day 4

1. old	5. hour
2. half	6. steak
3. gold	7. sugar
4. clothes	8. parents

Week 7 — Day 5

1. move
2. leave
3. brave
4. deserve
5. prove
6. solve
7. give
8. cave
9. lives

Week 8 — Day 1

1. p**ear**	6. ch**air**
2. sk**ir**t	7. hamm**er**
3. h**air**y	8. n**ur**se
4. sc**are**	9. b**ear**d
5. th**ir**sty	10. b**ur**glar

Week 8 — Day 2

1. Mr Brown coach**es** them.
2. They play match**es** each weekend.
3. The girls are playing against the boy**s**.
4. Karen throw**s** the ball.
5. Jack tr**ies** to grab it.
6. Natalie catch**es** the basketball.
7. Peeta worr**ies** that the boys will lose.
8. He watch**es** as the girls score again.

Week 8 — Day 3

1. careless
2. restful
3. speechless
4. forceful
5. helpless
6. fearful
7. joyless
8. playful
9. hopeful

Week 8 — Day 4

1. She has to h**old** on tightly.
2. She goes **every** week.
3. Sometimes she falls on the f**loor**.
4. But she always gets up a**gain**!
5. Tess thinks climbing is g**reat**.
6. She is p**retty** good at it.
7. Her f**ather** is proud of her.

Week 8 — Day 5

1. movement
2. illness
3. treatment
4. cleverness
5. silliness
6. payment
7. shyness
8. messiness
9. argument

Week 9 — Day 1

1. ✔	6. ✔
2. ✘	7. ✘
3. ✔	8. ✔
4. ✘	9. ✘
5. ✔	

Week 9 — Day 2

1. Tabitha w**a**nts a pony for her birthday.
2. The jelly is very w**o**bbly.
3. Gina walks tow**ar**ds the dog.
4. The cake is w**o**nderful.
5. "This is the w**or**st day ever!" shouted Sam.
6. Lara ate an enormous qu**a**ntity of sweets.
7. The witch was rew**ar**ded for saving a fairy.
8. The ring is w**or**th a lot of money.
9. The qu**a**lity of Kwame's art is amazing.

Week 9 — Day 3

1. b**oi**l	6. n**oi**se
2. **oy**ster	7. vo**y**age
3. p**oi**nt	8. cowb**oy**
4. j**oy**ful	9. p**oi**son
5. t**oi**let	10. destr**oy**

Week 9 — Day 4

1. Mike's
2. helmet's
3. scooter's
4. Paige's
5. go-kart's
6. boy's
7. James's
8. class's

Week 9 — Day 5

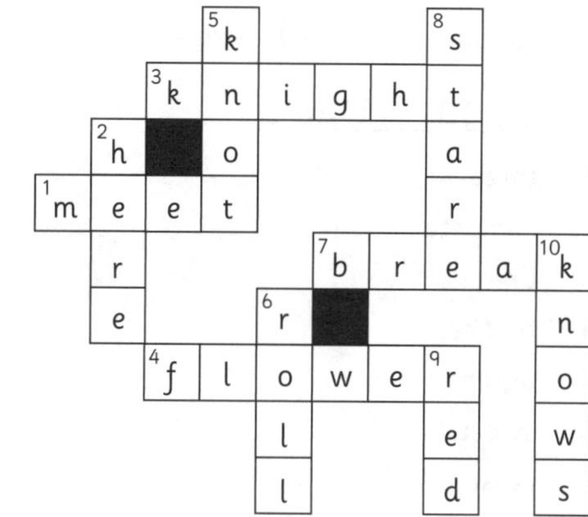

Week 10 — Day 1

1. There is **nothing** in the jar.
2. I went shopping the **outher** day.
3. On **Munday**, Pete goes swimming.
4. A friendly **woman** smiles at me.
5. The birds fly **abov** our heads.
6. My grandparents **come** for lunch.
7. Sharon's birthday is next **munth**.
8. The **ovn** burns everything.
9. Fran **discovered** some treasure.
10. Our chickens laid a **duzen** eggs.

Week 10 — Day 2

1. There is a fic**tion**al show on.
2. It's about an inva**sion** of dogs.
3. Their ambi**tion** is to take over the world.
4. There are lots of explo**sion**s.
5. One of the dogs loses his vi**sion**.
6. He might need an opera**tion**.
7. But the vet rubs in some lo**tion** and the dog is cured!
8. It is a very emo**tion**al show.

Week 10 — Day 3

1. Will loves **hiking**.
2. Hetty **chatted** to Stu.
3. Flo is **worried** about falling.
4. Duong is **braver** than Alice.
5. Kat **carried** some leaves.
6. Nick is **balancing** on a log.
7. This is the **prettiest** flower.
8. Felix is **planning** an adventure.
9. The tree is **bigger** than Diane.

Week 10 — Day 4

1. duck
2. pencil
3. camera
4. cactus
5. cuddle
6. bouncy
7. locket
8. kettle
9. cymbals
10. karate

Week 10 — Day 5

1. three
2. compete
3. dreams
4. teaches
5. agrees
6. sweet
7. reason
8. cheeky
9. these

Week 11 — Day 1

1. One **afternoon**, we went to pick some.
2. They gave us **wooden** baskets to put them in.
3. I wanted to pick a **thousand** strawberries.
4. My cousin spotted a **narrow** path.
5. Then, he **found** the biggest strawberry ever!
6. It was **enormous**.
7. It wouldn't fit **indoors**.
8. A **crowd** of people came to see it.
9. My cousin was very **proud**.

Week 11 — Day 2

1. He has **countless** things in there.
2. He is **hopeless** at sorting it out.
3. "All this stuff is **worthless**!" says Sophie.
4. "It's **priceless**," replies Mr Benson.
5. "No, it's **useless**!" argues Sophie.
6. "That piano is **tuneless**."
7. "It's why the till is **penniless**," she shouts.
8. "At least that spider is **harmless**," mutters Mr Benson.

Week 11 — Day 3

1. Ismail made some p**ie**s.
2. The sk**y** is dark at night.
3. Jacqui t**ie**s her shoelaces.
4. Those t**igh**ts are stripy.
5. Pippa makes a fr**ie**d egg.
6. Jesse likes the p**y**thon.
7. Romie s**igh**ed tiredly.

Week 11 — Day 4

1. Her **staury** is about a cowboy. — **story**
2. One **morening**, he goes outside. — **morning**
3. He gets caught in a **stawm** — **storm**
4. The rain is **auful**. — **awful**
5. He runs into a barn **befor** he gets wet. — **before**
6. He stays there until **dorn**. — **dawn**
7. He needs **mor** waterproof clothes. — **more**

Week 11 — Day 5

1. rice
2. celery
3. juicy
4. spicy
5. decide
6. medicine

Week 12 — Day 1

1. Sonia's cake looks amazing.
2. She's iced it beautifully.
3. The baker's son made cupcakes.
4. He'll decorate them later on.
5. I've made chocolate chip cookies.
6. You're all great at baking.
7. I haven't tried those tarts yet.
8. Jess's brownies look yummy.
9. I won't have one — I am too full!

Week 12 — Day 2

1. The mo**tion** of the boat made me ill.
2. The loca**tion** of the play is a city.
3. The lord and lady live in a man**sion**.
4. Ten**sion** is building at the contest.
5. Laila's ver**sion** of the story is very funny.
6. My posi**tion** in hockey is goalkeeper.
7. The nurse gives Jamie an injec**tion**.
8. There was a colli**sion** in the car park.
9. Juan is waiting at the train sta**tion**.

Week 12 — Day 3

1. She tiptoed **quietly** so he wouldn't hear her.
2. But **suddenly**, she stepped on a twig.
3. It snapped **loudly** with a crack.
4. "Who's there?" shouted the dragon **angrily**.
5. "Surprise!" laughed Helen **playfully**.
6. The dragon hugged his friend Helen **tightly**.

Week 12 — Day 4

1. darkness
2. useful
3. statement
4. successful
5. weakness
6. disagreement
7. appointment
8. delightful
9. dizziness

Week 12 — Day 5

1. Jeff **tuld** Tina he was bored. — **told**
2. He walked away from the **paff**. — **path**
3. He got lost in the long **gras**. — **grass**
4. Jess was **shur** the trail was over there. — **sure**
5. He's been lost for the **passt** hour. — **past**
6. **Evriebody** is looking for him. — **everybody**
7. Then Jeff's mum **fynds** him! — **finds**

E2SWSU11